The proven meth
to scale your business in Europe

THE 4 STEPS

TO GENERATE YOUR FIRST

MILLION EUROS

IN SALES

CHRISTELLE DAMIENS

First published in 2020 by Christelle Damiens

© Christelle Damiens 2020

The moral rights of the author have been asserted

All inquiries should be made to the author.

A catalogue entry for this book is available from the National Library of Australia.

ISBN: 978-1-925921-31-1

Printed in Australia by McPherson's Printing
Project management and text design by Michael Hanrahan Publishing
Cover design by Peter Reardon

The paper this book is printed on is certified as environmentally friendly.

Disclaimer: The material in this publication is of the nature of general comment only, and does not represent professional advice. It is not intended to provide specific guidance for particular circumstances and it should not be relied on as the basis for any decision to take action or not take action on any matter which it covers. Readers should obtain professional advice where appropriate, before making any such decision. To the maximum extent permitted by law, the author and publisher disclaim all responsibility and liability to any person, arising directly or indirectly from any person taking or not taking action based on the information in this publication.

CONTENTS

INTRODUCTION

Why this book

When I wrote my first book, I had in mind a small business owner wanting to get started in the European market. *Ready, Tech, Go! The definitive guide to exporting Australian technology to Europe* is a guide that gives a snapshot of why small business owners should consider Europe and what they should do to prepare for success.

For this second book, I wanted to ramp it up and go in depth in the methodology we have developed over the years at Exportia and that has proven to be successful for our customers. This book will be a long-term companion for the exporter, from initial sales to building a multi-million euros business.

My goal in this book is to break our method down into major steps for a small business to take and reach their first million euros in sales, and go beyond.

For those who have not read my first book, my world of export started with driving 10,000 km a month in Europe through to doing a Paris/Frankfurt–Sydney flight once per month. That's my export career in a snapshot.

I started in this extraordinary industry 20 years ago. From a corporate sales job in Paris in the IT industry generating 40 million euros per year, to scaling Australian technology businesses to their first million euros in sales Europe-wide, I have now become obsessed with one purpose: making as many small businesses in the B2B sector reach their first million euros in sales.

For this second book, I wanted to go in depth into the methodology we have developed over the years at Exportia and that has proven to be successful for our customers. This book will take you through four major steps to take your business to success in Europe.

I have come across hundreds of small businesses since I founded Exportia in 2006. And combined with solid corporate experience, as well as experience in export for a small business, I have noticed that the small and medium-sized businesses we come across always make the same mistakes. Here are some of the most common ones:

- Small businesses often have a short-term approach in Europe: 'Let's try it and see what happens.' If they don't succeed after six months, they give up. Sometimes they also give up because they run out of cash, not having anticipated that the results won't come instantly. Europeans take a long-term approach in business; they need to see you again and again.

- Early-stage companies intend to sell to Europe without having built a track record, whereas European buyers will only purchase from you if others have done so.

- Small and medium-sized companies tend to appoint the first European distributor that comes to them, without due diligence. It usually takes a few years for them to realise if this distributor is a waste of time.

- I have seen companies appointing a very large Europe-wide distributor with exclusivity. But it is often the case that large multinationals have their own agenda. They are hard to move, and difficult to exit from.

- One of the mistakes that can be the most costly is hiring a full-time employee based in Europe too soon. Even though it sounds logical, hiring in Europe to get that market going without having some experience in the European market is actually a bad idea. Small businesses starting in Europe often recruit a salesperson based in England, treating Europe as a whole block, while not knowing exactly which country will pick up in sales first. They end up with an English salesperson trying to get sales off the ground in France. Unsurprisingly, it does not work.

These common mistakes are just a few from a longer list. And these mistakes result in years of delay in getting to a good result. Taking your business to its first million euros in sales as fast as possible and with the lowest risk possible for your business is our utmost priority at Exportia. And this book will train you in our methodology, so that you can implement it in your business.

How this will unfold

The way we are going to achieve this together in this book will be by breaking down our methodology for you. I will first take you through our seven mission-critical export pillars. Our seven pillars are the key areas you always need to look at. They are key success factors for small and medium-sized businesses in Europe. Depending on which stage you are at in your business, whether you have a mature business or you are a start-up, or whether you are an experienced exporter or a newcomer in Europe, you will need to focus on different pillars.

These seven mission-critical export pillars are:

1. Product

2. Customers

3. Country

4. Sales channels

5. Marketing

6. Team

7. Dashboards

In the first seven chapters of this book, I will go through each of the seven pillars in depth. The great thing about this structure is that at any time in your export journey, if you have any difficulty, you can easily go back to the specific chapter related to your issue.

In chapter 8, every piece of the puzzle will come together into our 4-Step methodology to get you to your first million in sales.

Chapter 8 will take you step by step through our process. The objective is to de-risk each step, so you can proceed confidently into the next step having the information you need to justify going further and investing further financial and human resources in your expansion in Europe.

Chapter 8 will guide you along each step. It will explain what to do when, according to the stage you are at.

First, I will take you through the **Export Readiness Diagnostic**. This is the first step. This is where we check if your business is ready to export to Europe. If you are not ready, we go through a list of actions you should undertake to get ready.

The second step is our **Market Validation**. During this second step, I help you define your top two European countries to target. And in these top two European countries, I show you how we obtain feedback from key potential distributors or channel partners and key end-users. All of this information helps us validate that there is a market for your business in Europe. In this way, we can confidently proceed to the next stage with the right strategy.

In our third step, we roll out the strategy as defined in the Market Validation. This third step is a **Lead Generation** phase. In this stage, our aim is to get your first sales. We generate leads and focus on getting your first trials. At the same time, we want to secure your sales channel to lock in the sale.

Once we have generated enough leads and ideally your first sale, we focus on reaching your first million euros in sales and beyond. This is our fourth step, called **Scale**.

I have broken it down into several sub-stages. The reason is that you need to focus on specific mission-critical Export Pillars when you are just signing your first deals, and your focus will be different when you are scaling your European sales beyond one million euros.

My objective for you in this book

My objective with this book is to get as many small and medium-sized businesses on their way to their first million euros in sales, and to help them go beyond. I also want this book to be a methodology that businesses can refer to at different stages of their development. I have included templates and tools to make it as practical as possible.

I am excited to think that potentially every business owner or export manager could take their business to one million euros and beyond. Having seen the transformation of businesses that work with us over the years, going from zero sales in Europe to multi-million euros, I could not be happier if this book could contribute to scale more businesses. It de-risks a small business to have their sales spread over several continents. It makes them more attractive for investors. Small and medium-sized businesses successful in Europe create jobs and contribute to their own economy. I also love to see them compete successfully against large multinationals. This is one of my points of pride when we work with our clients.

Tech and me

Our methodology and my business at Exportia are very much focused on technology businesses. We have focused on small and medium-sized businesses mainly in business to business (B2B) in the following sectors: advanced manufacturing, electronics, machinery, medical devices, biotechnology, green technologies, software, cloud-based solutions and digital.

Our seven mission-critical Export Pillars and the 4 steps have been developed based on our track record in these industries.

If you are in the consumer goods sector, you may not find this methodology 100% suitable to your export project. Marketing to consumers requires different mechanisms that you won't find in my book. However, I am convinced there is plenty of templates, advice and content in this book that will still make it a useful read for your business.

1 | PRODUCT

Focus, protect, comply, and position your product

In this chapter we cover important aspects about your products. First of all, we get you to focus on the products that have the best chance of success in Europe. Throughout the book you will see that the word 'focus' comes up many times, because being focused is an effective way to succeed. Then another important factor is compliance. Europeans won't buy your product if you don't comply with their norms and standards, full stop. After that, we look at the ways you should consider protecting your intellectual property. (The good news is that Europe is usually a safe place when it comes to intellectual property.) Then we look at shipping and price lists. It will get quite hands on, as I will provide some practical examples. Following pricing, I start to help you prepare for your first interaction with European clients: you will need to formalise how you position your product against your competition. And finally in this chapter, I'm going to take you through the elements that go with a product: aftersales, maintenance and user manuals.

So, first let's look at the factors you must consider when choosing what products to sell in Europe.

Focusing on the right products

How many products should I sell in Europe? And which ones should I pick?

If you have quite a broad range of products, you may wonder which product to pick to begin your expansion into Europe. There are a few criteria you should consider. First of all, it's always better to pick the product that has the best credentials in terms of quality. Your number one seller is a good start, because you would have a large number of customers and even case studies you could draw on when entering the European market.

A great thing with a mature product is that you would have had time to fine tune any quality issues. The first question a European client will ask is: who else is using it? Nobody wants to be the first. European customers will be reluctant to buy a product with little track record. The difficulty with brand-new products is their lack of history in terms of fault rate and quality. Even if a new product is beautifully manufactured, or software is well developed, until it's been used extensively you can't really 100% guarantee the quality of the product. And European clients won't take the risk of letting go of their current trusted supplier to take on a brand-new product with no track record.

Another difficulty with new products, with which you have limited experience, is that you won't be able to use customer testimonials.

You may also have received some European enquiries about a specific product of yours. And that is a good hint at the level of interest from the European market.

Another consideration is a product's ability to meet European standards. We will talk about that later in this chapter. It's important for you to choose a product that either is already compliant with European norms and standards or that can easily pass the standards with a little work.

If you are just entering the European market for the first time, I would suggest you focus on a limited number of products, or even just one to begin with. An important factor to consider is the cost of commercialising a very large range of products in Europe to start with. If you want to start commercialising 20 products, you may have to multiply a number of costs by 20; for example, the cost of trademarking a product name, or of translating a product manual. It's also more intensive to train a distributor's sales team on 20 products rather than one or two products. You will achieve quicker results from a European distributor if you get their attention focused on just one or two specific products to start with.

When launching products in Europe for our clients it's typically quicker for us to generate the first sales for a limited number of products. Once we have developed the relationship with European clients and distributors, we can then offer additional items. It's also easier to gather feedback about one or two specific products rather than 20.

Typically, the general rule we observe is to generate sales as fast as we can, be successful with that first experience, and then we can expand the range we sell. This is also more cost effective for our clients.

If you really have no idea which product you should choose, the best way to decide is to run a field test. Target a few European customers and distributors and ask them for their feedback about several products, and ask them to choose the most interesting product according to them. We conduct this type of testing for clients. It is quite efficient, but the project needs to be positioned for the clients and distributors you contact as a research exercise, particularly if your product is not compliant yet or if you have not defined the pricing yet.

The many ways to protect your intellectual property

Protection of intellectual property is vital, but it can also be challenging. On one hand, a lawyer is going to advise you to protect *everything*. This will definitely be the safest approach. There are different ways to protect your intellectual property overseas. An intellectual property lawyer can advise on this.

On the other hand, you have your budget constraints. Protecting every component of your intellectual property in every single European country is costly. But protecting nothing and hoping for the best is risky. So, you must assess what part of your IP portfolio is worth protecting. And are there specific geographical areas that are worth more to your business than others; for example, the German market might be bigger for your business than Bulgaria. How will this affect your approach?

What do you protect, how and why?

Generally speaking, Europe is a safe place to do business

I have to say that during 20 years of doing business in Europe, I have probably seen intellectual property issues only on two occasions. On one occasion, an Australian medical company we helped to enter the French market did identify a competitor headquartered in a small country in Eastern Europe that was commercialising a similar product in terms of functionality. They pinched the brand name of my Australian client and used it to commercialise their product in Europe. After an evaluation of the size of this competitor, the business owner found that this business was so small it did not represent any danger to them conducting business in Europe. My client's company name was also their brand name, therefore he felt that their brand was highly recognisable. The business owner made the decision not to trademark the brand name in Europe.

Up till now I can report that my client's business endeavour in Europe has not been negatively impacted by this small player. Our advice at the time was still to register trademarks in the European Union. However, my client's business was fairly small and they did not really have the resources nor the ambition to go strong in his development in every single European market, so they did not register.

Another example is a client of ours in the electronics industry. They have aggressive European expansion goals. They also put a strong emphasis on building their intellectual property portfolio. Hence, they really made sure they protected their brand name with a registered trademark in every single European country. They went through the trademark registration process. This registration process is publicly advertised, and companies may object to the registration. And this is what happened. A UK company had registered that brand name but for a different product. So, to get around that they had to specify along with their brand logo the product category they fit into. And they then gained the ability to market their product in the UK under that brand name.

For a non-European company, there are two ways to register your Trademark:

1. The European Union Intellectual Property Office allows you to register via a single registration process and at a single place a single trademark that covers all member states. The Fast Track process has the advantage of being a cost-effective and quicker way to register and manage your Trademark in one place. However, if your company is not registered in the European Union, you must have a valid representative. Check the full conditions of eligibility for the Fast Track registration process.[1]

2. If the country where your company is registered is part of the Madrid Protocol, you can register your trademark in the European Union or in the chosen European country(ies) this way. There are 106 members in the Madrid union at the time of writing.[2]

Let's now look at protecting your brand. The way to do this is to trademark a name, a logo and/or a slogan. And don't forget to trademark the logo as well as the actual words naming the brand. I realised a few years ago I had always trademarked my logo but not the actual word 'Exportia'. So, I trademarked the word. Interestingly, soon after I did, a gentleman contacted me to offer to cooperate as he found that there were some synergies between our businesses. He owned a competing business to mine. It was quite new. It struck me that he used a similar brand name to mine but added an additional word to it. I had all my IP registrations ready for a lawyer to look at, and we asked him in an e-mail to stop using this brand name. It was solved very rapidly.

In that case, the danger was that this person could create confusion in the market, and my clients and prospective clients could be misled into thinking that his business was part of mine. Having been active in the market for almost 13 years, he could have piggy-backed on my reputation, credentials and my 13 years of hard work!

---

1   https://euipo.europa.eu/ohimportal/en/fast-track-conditions
2   Check if your country is a member of the Madrid protocol: https://www.wipo.int/madrid/en/members/

Do I protect a product name or a company name?

A question you may have is: do I protect my company name or my product name? Well, this is a marketing question and a commercial one as well. You need to ask yourself, will I mainly be known under my company name? Or through my product name? Or are they both equally strong? You may decide that your product brand name is actually what you sell and your company name does not matter so much.

Funnily enough, in my client portfolio I have both cases. I have companies with a strong company name brand value, as it has a strong reputation and customers mainly know that their company name means quality products. Their product names are not as strong, and look more like product references. So in that case, it is easy: the focus is on trademarking their company name across Europe.

In other cases, I have clients that have a weak company name. Such companies are mainly known by their products, to the extent that customers tend to only call them by their product name. In these cases, clearly the product brand name has been carefully protected.

The choice of category under which you register your brand is also important, to make sure that at a minimum in your own industry nobody else can use your name.

Register what most matters to you: your brand logo, and name (the actual word or expression), and maybe your slogan or a motto if you have one. You want to pick and choose what is relevant to you and what you think is important to protect for your business.

What is at stake is to make sure that no one prevents you from conducting your business and reaching your revenue targets in Europe.

In which countries should I protect my brand?

One aspect of trading in Europe is making a decision on how many countries you would like to protect your brand in. There is a convenient system called the Madrid Protocol, which enables you to register a trademark in every single country in the European Union at once. I find this quite cost efficient for companies that are serious about the EU market and want to grow their business there, and are planning to stay and thrive in the European market in the long run.

It's also something to consider for companies that are building their business for an exit. You will get a better deal when selling your business if you can demonstrate your business and its intellectual property are well protected. It shows potential investors or buyers you have kept the competitors away.

Another reason for registering in the entire EU is that the European market is quite open. EU members trade with each other to a large extent. It is very common that – for example – a Belgian distributor will also have subsidiaries and teams in the Netherlands. You will see that an Austrian business will also be active in Switzerland, and the reverse is also true. In addition, if you target European multinationals, you will quickly realise they have factories throughout Europe. Of course, you may want to do business with them as well. For these reasons, in many cases it really makes sense to register trademarks Europe-wide.

As far as the UK is concerned, depending on how Brexit unfolds, you may have to register your trademark in the UK separately. At the time of writing this book, negotiations between the European Union and the United Kingdom are still in progress. It is unclear how the UK and the EU will collaborate in this field. If you have trademark registered in the UK or are planning to register in the UK, I would recommend you to check the latest UK government information.[1]

Let's consider if your business has financial constraints and you don't have the budget to register your trademark in every single EU country. What smaller businesses usually do then is they will focus in the first instance on one or two European countries. This will allow them to get a faster return, and it's more cost effective to develop one market at a time. It is very easy to just register your trademark in the market you are active in as a minimum. Or another way to look at it is to identify your top five European markets and to register in these five countries in the first instance. In chapter 3 about assessing countries and in chapter 8 about the

---

[1] https://www.gov.uk/guidance/eu-trademark-protection-and-comparable-uk-trademarks

Four Steps, I will share with you how to select the best European markets for your business.

Should I hire a lawyer to register trademarks in Europe?

Yes, you should. Intellectual property lawyers will have the capability to screen the market for companies that have registered similar trademarks. It is important for you to detect sooner rather than later that someone else is using your brand name or can prevent you from selling under your brand name.

A lawyer can also check if your brand can actually be trademarked. They will go through an assessment process with you: is your brand name too generic? Can you make it more specific? Or more unique?

Protecting your innovation before you launch in overseas markets

Patenting: keeping the competitors away

The aim is to keep your competitors away. Therefore, you should have protected your product or system innovation before you launch in Europe. For most companies that have global ambitions this is very often part of the product development process. Research and development (R&D) teams need to assess in the innovation process what can be patentable.

In this process, you will also assess how fierce your competition is and where your competitors come from. This is essential for you to precisely define your positioning versus your competitors.

In addition, you can make sure you don't infringe on anyone else's intellectual property. This protects you from future trouble, particularly if you are competing with large multinationals as they have the financial means to defend their rights.

To protect your innovation and evaluate your competition, your R&D team may, if appropriate, elect to patent your technology. This is extremely valuable. You protect your work, but you will also gain a very thorough competition analysis during the patenting process. Your intellectual property lawyer will assess which European and other international players have registered patents in your field and what unique parts of your product innovation you could register. The Patent Cooperation Treaty (PCT) enables applicants to register their patent in a large number of countries simultaneously.

When registering a patent, a critical step is to lodge it prior to communicating any information to the market. The timing is important for your product launch in Europe. Intellectual property lawyers will guide you through the process. If the process has been conducted the right way, you can confidently talk about your product when the innovation is patent pending. You can state in your communication that it's patent pending.

Other ways to protect innovation

Some of my clients have decided not to go through the patent process, or were not able to. They have either decided to keep their innovation secret, or – as with one of my clients – they are playing in a very niche industry. That client thought that the cost for him to patent was too high and the risk of any new competitor coming into the industry was low. He is in the plastics industry, and he also judged that the barriers to enter the market were high given the investment cost to get their mould fabricated.

Another client of mine was not able to patent one of the products that was going to be his number one seller. The reality is that his product is far superior to the competing products: it's smaller, lighter, and the performance is way above the competition. So, not patenting has never been an impediment to their commercial success.

Besides patents and trademarks, you can also use copyright to register the expression of an original idea. This is especially useful in the service industry. The service does not have a physical product to sell and protect. Therefore, it is all the more important to protect ideas with copyrights. You may also register the design of your product, as in its physical appearance. This is called a 'registered design'.

The most critical element for your success is to stay current and to keep innovating. And this can be a strategy of protection against the competition in itself. One of my clients is competing against multinationals. They were newcomers to a market dominated by large multinationals, but there had not been any innovation in their market for the last 20 years. So, this newcomer is growing very quickly because not only have they introduced a major innovation but they also keep introducing innovations at a very fast pace. They are blowing away the whole market, and they are working on staying ahead of the game. Their IP strategy is a mix of different elements, but the key to their success is that they keep innovating, and the speed at which they introduce new products to the market is phenomenal.

One of the first questions you'll be asked in Europe: do you comply with EU norms and standards?

Compliance is a legal obligation

Another element that's critical when launching a new or existing product in Europe is compliance. The European Union has a harmonised standards system. It enables you to be compliant with one single standard throughout Europe. Assume that you will have a standard to comply with. Again, use professionals to confirm which norms and standards you need to comply with for your products and what the process is. One of the most broadly used standards is CE Mark.

Ideally you want to use a consultant to check this out for you, unless you have a person who is competent in this area in house who can check the requirements. But I'm always a supporter of paying for the right resources to get the right information. This is a worthwhile investment.

In terms of the impact of Brexit on the standards, at the time I write this book this is not determined. Two outcomes are possible:

- at a certain point, you will have the obligation to comply with UK requirements that would have been developed just for the UK

- the UK may well negotiate a system of reciprocal compliance with a number of countries and with the European Union as well.

The first thing that a European buyer will ask you is: do you comply with the European norms and standards? If you don't comply you won't be able to sell. There is no point starting to make some efforts in the commercialisation process if your products do not comply.

Be conservative in terms of certification timelines when launching a product

In terms of timing, it's critical that you have a clear understanding of how strong your chances are of passing the European standards, and also the timeframes within which you will obtain your approval. You can maximise your chances of success as a product is at the design stage, ensuring that it complies to the European requirements. However, the time it will take the testing house to test your product and state whether it does comply with the European requirements is *not* under your control. These certification bodies may have long waiting times. Or, your certification may fail.

The certification time must be taken into account in your launch plan. In this instance, underpromise and overdeliver. There is nothing worse than promising a given launch date to a sales team that will be excited to talk about a new product and will then be disappointed to announce that the product is not quite ready.

Do I need an authorised representative in Europe?

From time to time, depending on your product and if you don't have a subsidiary in Europe, you will be asked to have a local representative in Europe. Very often the role of this local representative is simply to hold all the documents that prove your products comply with the local European requirements.

This is particularly important in the medical sector, where the authorities want to make sure that in the event of any issue due to the use of a medical product, they can rapidly get hold of the product and company details and access any information they would need. In case of any problems, the first question will be: 'Please provide all documents to demonstrate that you are compliant with the European requirements.'

Some clients ask me if they should give this responsibility to their distributor. Personally, I always like my clients not to depend too much on their distributors. I would recommend keeping the authorised representative strictly independent; this way you have full freedom to appoint additional distributors, and to also stop working with a distributor if you need to. At Exportia, we have taken that role on a couple of occasions.

Shipping to Europe: (mostly) a no brainer

In almost 20 years of being in the export industry, I've never had any major issues in shipping things to any European country. It comes down to having the right freight forwarder. They can guide you through the process and documentation. Freight forwarding is a very competitive market, so you have plenty of options.

Let's look at some of the things you should be aware of.

Always specify the 'Incoterm' in a quote

Whether you are in a price-sensitive market or not, or if your product is quite large, the cost of shipping to Europe from your location may be an important element in your quote.

It's quite easy to get an estimate of this. Any freight forwarder would easily price several options for you. It is an interesting exercise for you to do in order to understand the total price landed at your clients' location, and whether you price your products 'ex-works' or not. Ex-works is an international term that defines what the shipping terms are. It is an 'Incoterm' (international commercial term). You need to specify the Incoterm you choose when you prepare a quote or create a price list for your clients, to avoid misunderstandings.

The Incoterms specify who – either the buyer or the seller – is in charge of and will pay the following:

- the freight
- the insurance of the goods
- the customs clearance, which is the payment of the import duties, and local taxes, which is mostly VAT (value-added tax).

It will also specify at which location the responsibility for an item is handed over from the seller to the buyer. It may be the port, or a specific address.

As I write this book in 2019, the most favourable term for you as a seller is ex-works; this means the buyer will organise the pick-up from your factory and will arrange the delivery to their warehouse in their own country.

In 13 years of shipping goods from Australia to Europe, I have found that a few of my clients would not dare quoting ex-works. However, I always strongly recommend using ex-works. Then you can be more flexible. If you are dealing with a large distributor they would import an enormous amount of goods, so they may have better shipping deals than you have. Therefore, more often than not, it's worthwhile for them to organise the freight themselves.

For small goods, air freight is still the most convenient, especially if you are not in a price-sensitive market. You can consider sea freight instead of air freight either when your goods are quite large to ship or when the volumes are starting to get high. A different Incoterm needs to be used if you are shipping via sea.

I advise you to consult the latest Incoterm definitions, as they are changing in 2020.

A few things to prepare before talking to a distributor or a client

First, to be ready to have your first discussion with a prospective buyer, you need to know the delivery time to ship your product either by air or by sea, depending on the delivery mode you have chosen.

When giving a price ex-works to a buyer, she will ask you what the cost of shipping will be. It is then very handy to know roughly what percentage of the order value the buyer should add to work out her buy price and include shipping and import duties. For example, you would tell her shipping and import duties are a maximum of 5% of your order (of course it varies according to the size of the order). This is a good number to have in mind.

You can check the current import duties into the European Union on the TARIC portal.[1] For that you first need to check your International HS Code (as part of the Harmonized Commodity Description and Coding System). European Customs will calculate the applicable import duties according to your product category.[2] Each product is classified according to an International Product Classification. You need to find out which category your product falls into; it's quite an easy process.

If it's too hard to calculate a generic percentage, just do several simulations of shipping costs for three different-sized orders: for a small order, for a medium order, and for a large order. You can then give several examples to your buyer.

Another option that's also convenient to have prepared is a typical assortment for a first stock order for a distributor. That will help you give some examples to a new distributor you are talking to. It will enable you to give an example of shipping cost and import duties on a typical first order.

What I also usually like to know is the minimum order quantities (MoQ). This is something you would be aware of from dealing in your domestic market. When shipping internationally, you might need to make these MoQ a bit higher, to avoid excessive shipping costs.

When is the time to hold stock in Europe?

Having stock in Europe enables you to provide fast delivery to your European clients. This is a customer-friendly option. However,

---

1   European Union website: https://ec.europa.eu/taxation_customs/business/calculation-customs-duties/what-is-common-customs-tariff/taric_en.
2   Refer to definition by the UN: https://unstats.un.org/unsd/tradekb/Knowledgebase/50018/Harmonized-Commodity-Description-and-Coding-Systems-HS.

if you are still at the beginning of your development in Europe, I would still continue to push for a direct shipment from your factory, to avoid the cost of warehousing in Europe.

Your distributors will have to hold stock for you in Europe; this is what you should aim for. Clients will ask you where your European stock is, but believe me it's okay if you don't have stock in Europe, especially if you are shipping air freight. If a client refuses to buy from you because you don't have stock in Europe, you need to clarify if that is really the reason. It may hide another reason, so do investigate their motivation.

With most of my Australian clients, when they start to sell into Europe they ship from Australia to Europe direct. It usually takes 7 to 10 days air freight. A few times, major European distributors I have been dealing with mentioned that they were surprised how quick it was, and that the European competitors sometimes took longer to deliver from Europe itself! This is because the European competitors ship by road.

Having stock in Europe does not always make sense. However, in some instances you may not have any other option than having stock in Europe; for example, if your product needs fast delivery. In that case, you need to investigate which country would be the best location for your European platform.

Having gone through this process with several clients of ours, we found some very good options in Belgium and in the Netherlands. They are traditionally two hubs for European logistics. One of the reasons is the size of their ports: Antwerp and Rotterdam respectively. If you are shipping by container from your country of origin, both of these ports are good options. You can easily obtain quotes by asking for a list of third-party logistics providers from the Dutch and Belgian government agencies in your own country. They will be very happy to help. Get several quotes to assess and compare the cost of shipping.

For now, I would exclude the UK as a logistics hub if you want to be able to easily ship Europe-wide. There are some uncertainties as to whether goods shipped from the UK to Europe will encounter import taxes. It all depends on how the negotiations between the UK and the European Union go.

If there is a specific country inside the European Union with which you are doing a significant amount of business already then it could be cost effective to have your European platform based in that country. If your growth plan is large and Europe-wide, check several logistics hubs – and definitely include Belgium and the Netherlands in the mix.

Pricing your product for the European market

Setting a unique European recommended retail price list

The first step in the pricing process is to have your recommended retail price (RRP) in euros ready for you to use while discussing with a European customer as well as a distributor. This is the price that a European consumer or end-user of your product would typically pay.

This is also called the list price. This should be valid Europe-wide. There is so much communication between European countries that it would be very confusing for a Belgian customer to see that the Dutch have a different price to them. So, keep it simple and just have one price list. The British would typically want to have their prices expressed in pounds. But generally speaking everyone – even in Switzerland – is fine with euros. It does make your life easier as well to update only one price list instead of many.

And it needs to have a time limit – prices are typically valid for one year. Having a one-year validity makes it easy for your customers to not have to worry about constant changes in prices. This is particularly helpful for distributors as they usually update their prices on their catalogue only once a year.

If you commercialise through a network of partners or distributors, you cannot insist they sell at certain prices. It's illegal. But the recommended price list is a guide. This price list is also the starting point for you to then determine a margin level for your distributor.

I strongly recommend you state your recommended retail prices *excluding* VAT (value-added tax). It makes your life easier as different European countries have different VAT rates. You don't want to have to constantly update these for different countries. When selling to a European business, it's easier to prepare an offer excluding VAT, as companies claim VAT anyway.

If you are in the consumer goods industry, you will have to update these prices for them to include the VAT of each country. When you are selling to consumers, you have a legal obligation to display prices that include VAT, so that you don't mislead consumers.

The benefits of having the price list as a separate document

This price list should be publicly available

The idea behind having this price list separate from any special conditions or any distributor buy price is that you can share it without any risk. It is also a good way to start a conversation with a new distributor without sharing too much information at first.

The other important point is that it enables you to strongly encourage your distributor's sales representatives to sell to this price (even though it would be illegal to impose it on them).

This is simple to implement and so important

For one of my clients, we launched their product in France and Germany. As we recruited distributors, we had one single pricing document. This pricing table would include the distributors' buy price and the recommended retail price. It became a bit of an issue. We shared this price list with their central purchasing and not with the sales team. We assumed the central purchasing would do so.

The sales representatives would then check their buy price in their system, and add a margin to it to get their sell price. We ended up having to face major discounting issues as we found that the sales representatives were not informed enough about our recommended retail price. It created a lot of confusion, and we later decided to include in their pack during each training our recommended retail price as a standalone document.

Therefore, I now recommend having the price list as a separate document. It becomes really problematic when you launch a product in the market and its RRP is not what it should be because of price confusion.

I have noticed another advantage of keeping it separate. Very large distributors often have a purchasing division and the product management divisions that are mainly in charge of purchasing your product. Then they may even have a centrally operated logistics platform for the rest of the company. This logistics platform, being a warehouse and a dispatching centre, will have its own costs to cover. Therefore, the sales departments, run as separate divisions, will be 'charged' internally the cost of buying the product and the logistics platform costs as well. It means that a sales representative located in a region will not see your buy price but the buy price plus logistics costs that have been entered in his company's IT system. It means that if you show him your price list, and the price at which you sell to his head office, it might be confusing. It's not a big deal, but you want a salesperson to focus on the selling part. And all they should worry about is the price at which they are selling. So keep it simple while communicating to them and stick to RRP/list price. If they want to check their buy price, they can find it in their own company system and it is none of your business.

It's a common practice for very large distributors to control the prices used by their sales teams. They can, for example, communicate in their internal pricing system a higher buy price than their actual buy price negotiated by the purchasing department. This way the sales team has less room to use a low sell price, and overall for the distributors they maintain higher margins.

Your checklist for producing distributor price lists or client price lists

There are a few points that need to be very clear in your price lists for European distributors or clients. This very simple checklist will help you to create your own template, so you ensure there is no miscommunication. You can also see how I have laid it out in the price list example on page 23.

You should make this document as generic as possible, and avoid having too many special conditions, such as adding too many discount levels or special prices. You can instead, for example, supply the information for specific offers you would make in an e-mail. A price list needs to be simple and easy to understand.

Here are the items you should include:

- the Incoterm

- validity

- international HS code(s)

- distributor margin

- minimum order value (MoV) and minimum order quantity (MoQ)

- payment terms

- delivery time.

Let's have a look at each of these.

The Incoterm

First, specify the Incoterm in the price, so you and your customers are sure to understand each other. For example, '1,000 euros ex-works, Sydney, Australia' or '1,200 euros DAP, Lyon, France'.

Again, I strongly recommend having your price list expressed ex-works. With one of my clients, we were dealing with a major French distributor, and they were placing very large orders. To make it easy for them, we quoted in DAP (delivery at place), delivered to their city in France. This DAP pricing included my client's typical cost of putting an order together, and typical shipping costs for typical orders. Then a few months later, the French distributor started to request that we package the goods in a specific way: each item inside each box was to be labelled individually, each box should only include one product, and more.

The DAP price had been based on an optimal packaging of the products. For example, my client's logistics department would pack different products in one box to make sure they could optimise the cost of shipping. But with the new configuration asked for by the distributor, this was not the case anymore. Hence, the stated DAP prices were no longer so favourable.

That is why I like to always push for ex-works; it really maintains my client's best interests.

Indicate a validity and custom code

Because you are communicating your prices in euros, which may not be your home country currency, you want to give yourself the freedom to update your price list. So, make your price lists valid only for a certain amount of time. You always have to imagine that a price list will stay with a buyer for a long period of time, and you don't want a buyer to ask you for a specific price you gave them two years ago. Since then, your prices will probably have increased.

Also indicate your HS code, sometimes called a custom code. European customs will calculate the applicable import duties according to your product category.

This is quite handy for your clients to see in this document. Based on this HS code they can then calculate the cost of custom clearance.

Distributor margin

For a distributor's price list, you will need to calculate a distributor buy price. For that you need to work out which margin you are giving your distributor. In the sales channels section (chapter 4), we will talk in more detail about examples of negotiation strategies with distributors. Here in this section we focus on creating your standard price lists.

My recommendation is to have the same format and margin levels worldwide. Then you adapt and make specific conditions for each country. Therefore, in your standard distributor price list your pick a margin that is quite favourable to you. Let's take the example of 35% – you apply this figure to every distributor price list for every country you are dealing with. You can then use this 'standard' distributor price list as a starting point for a discussion with a new distributor, for example. It does not expose you too much. Then your distributor can obtain better pricing based upon good performance, such as reaching a specific sales target. This is to be negotiated. (Again we will talk about this more in chapter 4.)

Some of my clients have made the choice not to have distributor price lists as a way of minimising the risk of their distributor prices being seen by their competitors. The only pricing document communicated is their end-user RRP or list price. It's a choice for each company.

Minimum order value (MoV) and minimum order quantity (MoQ)

A buy price per item needs to correspond to a specific minimum order quantity (MoQ).

In some instances, if your products are packed in boxes of 10 products for example, you may prefer to indicate the MoQ for each product.

In addition, it may be convenient for you to add a minimum order value (MoV). For example, a distributor may order a minimum of 5,000 euros ex-works, San Francisco, US. This is good for you, as you can then cater for the cost of putting an order together. I have also seen some of my clients add an extra fee for any order below that minimum order value. This also encourages your distributor to place larger orders.

Payment terms

If you don't have general trading terms specified in any other documents or available on your website, you may want to specify them in your price list.

Payment before shipping is well accepted if you are dealing with a distributor or a client for the first time and it's their first order. After that, the generally accepted payment term is '30 days end of month'. The Italians will push it to 60 days; I think this is way too long if you are a small business, and 60 days on paper may well end up being 90 days. So, my advice is to keep your payment terms very tight and really stick to this. One of my clients added a very smart statement to their 30-day payment terms: 'We reserve the right to change payment terms if we notice late payments'. It's simple, and gives you the opportunity to put a regular late payer back to payment in advance.

Delivery time

It is also good to indicate generic delivery times by air and, if appropriate, by sea.

To protect yourself when stating a delivery time, you should include disclaimers. For example, one of my clients in the electronics industry states that the delivery time is subject to availability of electronic components, in case of a shortage at a global level.

Other clients like to state the given delivery time can't be guaranteed outside the usual quantities ordered. Imagine a scenario where a distributor that usually orders 90 units per month suddenly orders 500 per month. That's great, but you may not be able to ship in the usual 7 to 10 days, and will need a longer delivery time for such quantities.

When stating a delivery time, don't forget to factor in the typical time it takes your team to prepare an order, or production time if you don't have an item in stock.

What if I don't sell through a distributor?

If it's your strategy to sell direct to very large end-users, ideally you should quote your list price. If they generate such large volumes for your business that you would consider better prices than the list price, then you can formalise roughly the same format of price list as for a distributor.

However, the pricing level should still be slightly different. If you think that down the track this client might buy through a local distributor and not direct from you, you should make sure you have anticipated a margin for your distributor. When the time comes for a distributor to look after that client, the distributor can have its own margin.

Build your own distributor price list

It's now time to formalise your own distributor price list. At the following link you'll find templates in English, French and German, and you'll see an example below. Adapt them to your own context and trading terms: www.exportia.com.au/downloads

To establish your *recommended retail price* list, you will need to take off the word 'distributor' and remove the distributor price. Remember that the value-added tax (VAT) is different depending on the country. If you deal in B2B then you can formalise your RRP excluding VAT. For consumers, you will need to add the VAT.

[YOUR COMPANY LOGO]	NAME OF DISTRIBU-TOR/ PRICE LIST					
These prices are valid from 1 January 2019 until 31 December 2019						
Ref.	Description	HS Commodity Codes	Minimum order quantity	Ex-Works unit [City, Country] price	TOTAL	
Product Category 1						
xxx		000 000 000	50			
Product Category 2						
xxx						
xxx						
xxx						
Product Category 3						
xxx						
xxx						

Terms and conditions
Prices effective 1 January 2019 and valid until 31 December 2019 All prices are in Euros and do not include value sales tax All prices are Ex-works from our facility in [CITY, COUNTRY] Payment terms are 30 days from end of month. Note: [YOUR COMPANY NAME] reserves the right to change the payment terms for late payment.
Delivery times
For orders of [X] units or less, [YOUR COMPANY NAME] will have the order ready for dispatch within 7-10 days from receipt of the purchase order. For orders over this amount, [YOUR COMPANY NAME] will confirm the order time. Shipping time from [COUNTRY] are usually x - y days per airfreight and x- y weeks per sea freight.

Knowing how your product is positioned in the European market is critical to your success

Start with an in-depth competitor analysis

Whether you like it or not, your potential European clients will want to know where you stand in comparison to their usual supplier. They will want to compare product features and also prices. A really valuable exercise that will provide you with a lot of interesting market information is to conduct an in-depth competitor analysis.

First of all, if you do not know your competitors, or you don't think you have a comprehensive list, do some homework to ensure you have a comprehensive view of your competitors.

You are preparing yourself and your sales team for your first conversation with a European client. Do that first broadly for Europe, and then focus on the major competitors. As you get more familiar with the country you are going to focus on first, you will find out which competitors are the most present in that specific country and you will find new ones as you gain more knowledge of this specific market. To find out who your competitors are you can conduct a basic Google search using the European Google domains, such as google.de for Germany, google.co.uk for the UK, google.fr for France, and so on. Preferably get your product keywords in French and German to do your search. Don't just Google translate it – seek the assistance of a native speaker to get the best translation for your product in French and German. Then you should be able to find distributors active in Europe. You will find either their European webpage or their distributor's page.

Another really good approach is to check the list of exhibitors at major European trade shows in your industry. You will find competitors there. If you don't find any, you must have picked the wrong trade show.

Keep your list of competitors up to date. This is a good tool to share with sales teams.

Building your competitor review

Compare features

Draw on your knowledge of your domestic market to establish a list of features you can rate your product and your competitors' products on. Keep in mind what your customers typically look at when comparing your product with the competition.

Here are a few examples of features you could compare:

- power
- autonomy
- speed
- guarantee

- weight
- size
- price
- functionality.

These are your product's inherent characteristics. A great way for you to collect this information is to find your competitors' European product manuals: they would usually be multilingual so you should be able to find them in English.

Compare benefits

Then think about the benefits as well. In the early stage in the European market you may not know all your competitors' products benefits to start with, but you can use the following matrix to identify where you have knowledge gaps. Bear in mind that the benefits you find in your domestic market may be different in the European market.

One of my Australian clients had a great technology based on artificial intelligence that predicted water consumption at a large scale. One of the great benefits for Australian city councils was to be able to develop ways to save water, as Australia is prone to droughts. But when entering the European market, we found that water saving was not always a high priority of large cities in Germany, France and the UK. This was relevant in the south of France, Italy, Spain and Greece. We had to adapt our product presentation and focus on other capabilities of this product.

Examples of benefits include:

- ease of use
- fast deployment
- attractive look and feel
- versatility
- fast return on investment.

Always keep in mind that the benefits are perceived as important in the eyes of your customers. Therefore, rate your benefits based on what is important for the customer.

Compare price levels

In terms of pricing, list prices or recommended list prices are easily obtained on the web. This is very important information to obtain. It will give you a feel for the overall price level acceptance of the European market. This research will show you what the European market is willing to pay for your product category. It's extremely interesting to know if your market is used to buying your competitors' products at a high price. Or are they used to buying cheaply made products?

This information is really important to find out, because it helps us prepare our argument and value proposition when approaching a European customer. We need to be able to quickly assess if our client's product is outpriced or not. If our price is significantly higher, is that justified? Even if it *is* justified by great features and benefits, the question is then, will the Europeans buy it?

For instance, with one of our clients we had to change our approach. We initially focused on a product that had been developed for the Australian market. It was extremely robust to meet the Australian outback conditions, and it provided a lot of technical features to meet the needs of the savvy Australian end-users. It had so many great technical features that the product ended up being quite highly priced, and this could be totally justified.

However, when we looked at the European market, we found that the final customers who would be the target for this type of product were not savvy at all. They were used to a very simple interface, with very limited information. The potential partners were worried that the end-users would be confused by so much information. So even though my client had a far superior technology, the features and benefits that he typically would sell his product on did not work in Europe.

In addition, the product was much higher priced than what local customers were used to. We could not get interest because the additional features and benefits in comparison to the European competition had no value in their eyes. So we changed strategy and focused on a product that had better chances and better feedback.

Create a competition matrix

When you do a competition matrix, you can check where you are missing information. Fill in the gaps as you speak to customers and gain a better understanding of the European market. An example of a competition matrix is shown below.

	Your company	Competitor 1	Competitor 2	Competitor 3
	Product name	Product name	Product name	Product name
Feature				
Speed				
Guarantee				
Quality standard				
Benefits				
Ease of use				
Speed of deployment				
Price (RRP)				

Indirect competition is as important as direct competitors

When looking at competitors, don't underestimate indirect competitors as well as what I call 'in-house competition'. Indirect competitors may not offer exactly the same product as yours, but for one reason or another they might be what the local clients are used to. So, it's important for you to have a broad view of the indirect competition. It might be, for example, a product that offers only part of what you offer, or it might be manufactured in a different material.

For example, a client of mine is a designer of a manufacturing line. So, for this client, the indirect competition is for their clients to buy the finished goods, instead of buying the manufacturing line to be able to produce the finished goods themselves. The indirect competitor is the producer of finished goods. You would have to then explain how you differentiate and what the benefits are of manufacturing yourself, such as controlling your entire supply chain.

The other type of competition – called 'in-house' or 'internal competition' – is fairly common in the IT industry. If you are selling software to a company that has a large team of developers, they might think they are better off developing that software themselves instead of buying it off the shelf. In that case, the competitor would be the IT department of your client. I have found, for example, it's often quite hard to sell software to government organisations that have large teams of software developers. Typically, the manager of that department would want to 'keep the team busy' and not create the perception of any threat to their jobs.

How will aftersales and maintenance be managed?

Define what aftersales will look like for Europeans

In the commercialisation of your product, you should plan for your aftersales. This is particularly important for technology products and B2B sales. In the sales process, usually this question will come up with your client. And even if you have not fully established in detail how the product is going to be serviced during and after warranty, it is important to have a feasible plan in mind.

When you are starting in the European market and your product is manufactured outside Europe, the quality of your aftersales will be a critical factor for a buyer. If you get your first client, and they quickly find that you are very hard to deal with when it comes to aftersales, you will discourage them from continuing to buy your product. Clients of mine that adopted a very customer friendly policy and systematic replacement of a faulty product during the warranty period, without any trouble, were quite successful.

The replacement process should be very easy during warranty. It can help a lot to have a local partner or distributor that holds stock and can quickly replace a product.

You may also plan for a local technical partner, or if you have reached a significant level of sales it may be time to hire local technical support. You will find that for some types of clients it will be imperative that you have local technical support before they buy from you. You may need to plan for that to get a deal signed.

It is also important to establish a simple and efficient process to be able to track and monitor the progress of an aftersales request. There's nothing worse than being slow in responding to an enquiry, or not being sure where it is at.

Who should be in charge of aftersales?

This is a function that I typically recommend that your operations department takes over. The sales team in charge of Europe should be informed but not in charge of this. The issue we often found at Exportia, when we had to take on this function, was as the sales were quickly growing, we started to become overwhelmed with enquiries. As we have a sales team that typically travels a lot, we came to a point where we could not provide fast and efficient aftersales.

The logistics side of the aftersales should be handled by the operations team, for which it's typically the daily job to track and organise product replacements. They are also able to monitor and analyse these enquiries. When you are a small team of course your sales team can help, but as your sales grow they may not be the best people for the job. Sales teams should just sell.

Have an excellent aftersales system, and learn from it

A really good way to create an efficient aftersales system is to automate these enquiries. How easy it is nowadays to create a form on a website to collect these enquiries. You can set it up for e-mails to be sent to your operations team, and copy the salesperson in charge. What we have also done for a client of ours is we have translated these forms into several languages. It's great for us to be able to point either a client or a distributor's sales representative to this webpage to make sure they are looked after efficiently in their local language.

What's important is for the process to be simple, and it should be trackable. If you are quite far away, like most of our clients that are in Australia, you have to be smart and show you are responsive. That's why automation and the use of your website is definitely the way to go to reduce that distance with your clients. It's a way for you to be close to them. It's important, as you will compete with local European players, and they have the capability to provide very diligent aftersales and technical support.

Offer your European clients the use of your freight forwarder account to pick up faulty goods and to ship a new product. Don't make your clients pay for freight for faulty goods replacement, particularly when they are still under warranty.

Learning from faults is also valuable. It's very important for your business to track trends, and it's also important for your sales team to be kept in the loop. It's interesting for you to be able to capture the circumstances under which the product was used, to understand if there is anything specific about your European clients that you have not anticipated. Your sales team must be informed, as they are the ones facing the client and they are also your eyes in the field. They can train a client that does not know how to use your product well, and therefore finds that the product is faulty whereas perhaps it is not. Your sales team also needs to be able to keep the client informed on how the aftersales is being taken care of.

The same applies for your extended sales team: your distributors' sales representatives and/or your sales agents. You want to make it easy for them to keep getting sales from any clients that encounter a faulty product. If the customer service is bad, clients will stop buying.

Organising maintenance

If your products require maintenance, you also want to anticipate that process quite early. You may need to have a distributor trained to do your maintenance. If this is not possible, or you prefer an independent maintenance centre, you will need to identify one, and certify this company if that is part of your typical process. It's useful to look at what your competitors are doing in terms of maintenance; you want to make sure you provide very high value maintenance. Again, this is an opportunity for you to compete with local players.

We will dig more into the partnering models in chapter 4 of this book, dedicated to channels. But just a tip for you now: if you are using distributors and your product needs maintenance, you may find it convenient to train and certify one of your distributors as a maintenance centre. It's a good idea, and quite convenient. The only drawback is that, if you don't train all your distributors as maintenance centres, other distributors won't be happy handing over the maintenance of the products to a competitor.

Think about these issues when you do your investigations, and plan for an option that can efficiently service as many customers as possible.

Preparing a European user manual

Ideally have a multilingual manual

If you commercialise your product in the European market, you will need to have a user manual in the language of the country you are selling to. It needs to be packed with your product, if you have a physical product.

You can start just with the countries you are selling to: for instance, having your manual translated into French first if you are starting in France. Then, as you start your entry into the Italian market you will need to get it translated into Italian.

But, ideally you want to have a multilingual user manual pretty quickly. The first reason is that at the production level it may not be very convenient to place a French manual in the product to be sold to a French client and a German manual into the product ordered by a German client.

The other reason is that your distributors or clients may, more often than not, sell to several countries in Europe, and these European end-users will need a manual in their language. Many of my clients have asked me, do we really have to do that? Yes, you do. You want to be close to your customers and talk to them in their own language. It is a much better customer experience for them. And, most importantly, this is a legal requirement.

With some of my clients, we have selected the biggest potential countries and done the translation of the user manual into these languages first. We then added other languages as the distribution grew.

Making translations cost effective

When you have very comprehensive and lengthy manuals, it can be costly for you to get them translated into the 24 languages of the European Union. But, ideally, you probably want to sell to *all* these countries down the track, and therefore you will have to do these translations at some stage. Your European competitors will already have that sorted.

Here is the way translations work. You submit your document to a translator; always choose a native speaker, and forget about using a student to do that job. The legal implications of giving the wrong instructions to a client may be high and it's not worth the risk. Use a professional translator.

A translator will provide a quote based on the number of words. The more words the more expensive it will be. So, the trick to make it cost effective is to create user manuals that have a lot of visuals, and use as few words as possible. The extreme example is IKEA and their manuals; there is not a single word in them.

In addition, I would also recommend you find a good translator and stay with that translator if things go well. Nowadays, they use very smart software for their translations, and if they keep doing translations for you over and over, at some stage they should have gathered a lot of vocabulary from you that they can use over and over. Hence, your translations will get cheaper (as long as, to some extent, the same words and phrases are used repeatedly).

Don't hesitate to have the translations checked by your local distributor, and provide the translator with the feedback. A professional translator will research your industry to pick up the terminology, but it can still be a difficult process for them. Work in tandem with them, and if you provide feedback in a constructive way they will be able to take it into account.

This is how we work with our team of translators at Exportia. We as the sales team usually know the local terminology, and when the salesperson checks the translations she then shares it with the translator. Use your distributors as well; get their feedback on the manual you had translated into their language.

Providing your multilingual user manual

You can also try to save on printing costs. For example, if you think about the IT industry, when you buy a laptop you usually get it delivered with a 'quick set-up guide' to get you started. For more details you can go online to download a more comprehensive guide. This is a good way to save on printing costs. You can have a short multilingual user manual printed and shipped along with your product. And then in that guide you point your customers to your website for a more comprehensive guide in their language.

Checklist and templates you can prepare to set you up

As a summary for your Product Pillar, first pick one or two products that will be your focus to start with. Then for each product of focus:

Make sure your products comply with European regulations, so that they can be sold without any delay.	
Make sure each product is protected. Have an intellectual property protection strategy for each product of focus.	
Make sure you know your differentiators from competitors present in the European market. You can achieve that through a competition matrix.	
Make sure you have worked out your minimum order quantities per product.	
Make sure you have done a rough estimate on the percentage of your typical order value that would represent your cost of shipping and import duties. You can refer to TARIC[1], the European Union portal, to check import duties once you have worked out your HS code for your product.	
Establish a multilingual European recommended retail price (also called list price) or end-user price list for the European market, excluding VAT. The VAT rate may vary from country to country.	
Formalise your multilingual distributor price list with a conservative margin. This way you have your starting point for a discussion with a distributor. You may also want to add your main trading terms. Use the template provided. You may elect to only formalise a list price table, and formalise offers to distributors in a letter or an e-mail offer.	

All the editable spreadsheets in this chapter can be found on our website in the Resources section. Just go to exportia.com.au/downloads.

---

1   https://ec.europa.eu/taxation_customs/business/calculation-customs-duties/what-is-common-customs-tariff/taric_en

2 | CUSTOMERS

The key to your success in Europe

You should now have selected the top product or products you are going to focus on in Europe. Next it is time to look at your customers.

We will first identify who your buyer will be in Europe. At Exportia, we call it your 'ideal customer profile'. Then, we will examine preparing your approach to potential European customers. We will also look at your value proposition. After that, we will help you understand what a European buyer's perspective looks like. We will also look at the topic of selling to large multinationals. It's an important aspect to consider for small and medium-sized businesses. We will then address systems that will allow you to stay on top of your relationship with your European customers.

Prospective customers and customers are at the heart of your success in Europe. Your customers, and particularly your first European customers, should be your utmost priority.

Creating your ideal customer profiles

Focusing on one or two industries to accelerate sales

In this book you will hear the word 'focus' many times. And here it is again: you can accelerate your success in Europe by focusing on a limited number of customer targets.

Once you have selected your products of focus, you should concentrate on the type of clients that typically buy these products. These clients would typically be the clients that you know the best. They are your low-hanging fruit.

If you define the top two industries where your product, solution or software best performs in your home market, it will make it easier to identify the main European players in that field. It will then also be faster and cheaper for you to gain feedback from a handful of major players in those industries rather than interviewing customers in 15 different industries.

The reason I'm recommending you be focused is that it will be easier and faster for you to talk to a customer from an industry you already know, and where your products have a track record. Typically, European clients will be interested in knowing and monitoring what their overseas counterparts are doing. And that is how you can get a foot in the door in the European market. Starting with the customers you know best will accelerate your success in Europe.

At Exportia, our customers are small to medium-sized high-growth businesses. They need fast results and fast sales. This is why I have found this to be the best approach. Being focused allows us to quickly check whether that particular industry in Europe will respond positively to a product or not. We can then rapidly get an understanding of the effort it's going to take to enter the European market in this specific industry.

For example, for one of our Australian customers we decided to focus on two main industries in which they had previously had good references in their domestic market. They operated in the construction industry and the metal industry. It turned out that, in the French market, the construction industry was a particularly fast adopter of that technology. Our strategy was focused on that industry, and major sales were achieved in that area. As a consequence, one of our distributors, a small and agile one, decided to just focus on a sub-segment of that industry, where he found it was easy for him to get in: quarries. He worked very hard on that target, and was extremely successful.

In parallel, we caught the attention of the largest French distributor in the construction industry, and they found the product complemented their current range very well. With this focused approach, within two years we were able to generate millions of euros in sales, with a large part being generated in that industry.

When we approached the German market, we found the same success in the construction industry, but the metal industry prospective clients also showed keen interest. So we targeted both industries and obtained some good wins in both.

It was great for the management team and investors to quickly see that big European customers in France and Germany had adopted the product.

Defining your ideal customer profile to prepare for Europe

Before you instruct anyone on identifying your best potential clients, what I call the low-hanging fruit, you should create a comprehensive profile description of these clients. We find this particularly helpful when working with clients – we can make sure we are really hitting the right targets.

What you typically want to define are the types of organisations they are, whether they are public or private, and their industry. You will also need to define their size in terms of number of employees and/or turnover. It's also important to be very clear on the profile of the person(s) that are buying from you. You will define what their job role is, for example. (There is a template for this on page 184.)

Preparing your approach to potential European customers

Bullet-proofing your value proposition

You can articulate your value proposition on different levels. To start with you won't know your European clients well enough to have all the information you need. However, you can use your experience with your existing clients in your domestic market at the beginning. The clients you know best are the ones described in your ideal customer profile. They face challenges that your top products or solutions have helped them overcome. This is what you need to articulate.

I will now cover a set of issues you need to go through with your current customers that correspond to your ideal customer profile. It will help you formalise your value proposition. Then we will look at an example.

The problem, the solution and the outcome

The problem

First, you need to articulate what problem you solve for this profile of client. Just focus on the customer's pain here. Think of it in a clinical way: where does it hurt? Think about what keeps the client awake at night. Don't hesitate to use their jargon – use the industry language they would use to describe their problem.

It's valuable in this process to indicate who is feeling the pain. It's great to be able to articulate a value proposition at a department level or at a job position level. It gives much more impact when talking to a prospective customer. It's also easier for the client to relate to their own experience or the experience of their colleague.

The solution

Now it's time to explain what the solution is and how the problem is solved. Outline here why your product or solution is perfect to solve this issue.

The outcome

Then articulate the outcome or the end result for the client. If possible, explain it in terms of a business process that would have improved. It will have more impact if it's measurable.

An example value proposition

Here is an example of a value proposition for a specific company:

Client profile: Large construction company

Solution: Compact, light-weight protection device

The overall problem is: A new European safety regulation is imposing more drastic standards around protection of workers in quarries. Silica fibre, which is present in quarries, causes risks of silicosis. The company would like to make sure workers are protected against that risk.

At a high level, the management fears the risk of silicosis for their workers, and the risk of litigation resulting from that. They want to minimise risks by being compliant.

The safety department is in charge of making sure the company is compliant with this new regulation.

The site managers are also involved because they are the ones who will implement the new regulation on their construction sites. They have to make sure the workers actually wear the respiratory protections. They face a lot of resistance from their workers, with some actually refusing to wear protection because of discomfort.

The solution is: Client X's device is the smallest and lightest in the market. It does significantly increase comfort for the workers, and it also provides superior protection. In comparison to current solutions in the market, it is much easier to breath with this technology and it reduces fatigue. Workers can also enjoy the fresh air.

All these factors make it a great solution to implement, as this technology has a good level of acceptance. This allows compliance to be met.

The outcome is: Safety compliance has been significantly improved due to the adoption of the technology.

Examples of challenges faced by European industries

Over the last decade at Exportia, my team and I have come across numerous challenges faced by European industries. We have gladly helped to overcome these challenges with the solutions and products from our Australian clients. These challenges are often ongoing, and they can be faced by both companies and governments in the European Union. You may find some of these relevant for your target industry and products.

You need to know which challenges your product is solving. And you need to be able to articulate them. These challenges are your business opportunities.

Let's look at a few examples:

- Many European industries find it increasingly difficult to comply with stringent European environmental standards. They have to make sure they minimise their environmental impact. *This creates opportunities for low-emission, energy-efficient and green technologies.*

- The construction industry has to comply with safety laws for their workers. *This creates opportunities for better, more comfortable, smarter and connected protections for workers, training and compliance solutions.*

- Companies established in the European Union have to comply with consumer privacy and data protection laws. *This creates large opportunities for smart digital solutions to protect consumers, and to assist companies to comply and still run efficient marketing campaigns.*

- A major challenge today is to stay competitive globally by keeping costs down. *This means that any initiative or technology allowing companies to be more productive or make savings will definitely be of interest. Automation technologies will be a good solution for this problem.*

- European governments have encountered drastic budget reductions and now look at ways to make savings through digitisation. They also want to provide better service to their citizens. *This offers plenty of opportunities in new e-government services for citizens.*

The power of case studies

Formalising case studies is a great way to prepare for your discussions with potential clients. It's a powerful tool to create credibility when entering a new market where you don't currently have clients. Showing potential European clients your experience in their industry will be a great start.

You can develop your case studies following the same approach as your value proposition: the problem or initial situation, the solution, and the outcome.

Over the years, we have tested different types of case studies. We've found that video case studies have more impact than developing a flyer or a brochure. Case studies in a video are also great to showcase in your booth at a trade show, on social media and on your website. You can shoot a video, transcribe it, and then you also have a text version to use on your website or in a brochure. It can also be a great way to develop a photo library of clients' experiences with your product.

European clients will enjoy hearing about what their overseas counterparts are doing. On a global scale, companies often have contacts with their overseas colleagues, and these case studies can be a very powerful tool to build up your credibility level in Europe. When you work with a multinational in your home country and are looking at contacting this company in Europe, your case study again will be of great support. It will get you your first meeting much more easily.

As a minimum, it is advisable to have customer testimonials or customer references. Referees are great; your potential European customers would be happy to have a telephone conversation with them.

The European client perspective

Learn from potential negative feedback

There are a lot of advantages in quickly finding out if your usual 'favourite industries' are going to respond well to your product offering in Europe.

If they give you negative feedback, this should trigger some alerts for you to investigate why they aren't responding positively. You need to request their honest, detailed feedback on the reasons why they don't find your offer attractive.

Be aware that in some countries – such as Germany, Sweden, Denmark and Norway – you will get some very direct feedback. Don't take it personally; this is just the way businesspeople give you an opportunity to improve. If they have negative feedback, they won't hesitate to share. Southern Europeans may hesitate to do so, to preserve the relationship.

I am French and I personally enjoy working with the Germans because you know exactly where you stand, because they tell you directly. In France and other Southern European countries, you can get some honest feedback only once you have earned the trust of a person or you have developed a good relationship with them.

Be persistent in your investigation of what negative feedback means for your business. It will guide you to adjust your approach. Negative feedback may mean your competitor research is incomplete and/or you did not articulate your differentiators well enough. There is also a possibility that your potential European buyers do not require your product differentiators in comparison to what they currently have. In that case, it does not give them any incentive to change.

Let's take the example of one of my clients from the automotive industry. They manufacture an amazing product: the quality is superior to any competing items. But on paper, potential clients were not able to fully comprehend the value of the product, and buyers typically could not understand why the price was significantly higher than what they currently bought. However, we signed more deals once the clients had trialled the product. Once the end-users experienced the product, they could quickly measure the added value. That is how we won sales.

The cost of switching

When introducing a new product to the European market, you need to know what your prospective European clients are currently using. What equivalent product to yours do they use? They might be more or less happy with it. There will be a very strong reluctance to change to something new if the cost of switching to your product is too high.

Let me clarify what I mean by the cost of switching

Put yourself in a prospective customer's shoes for a second. They may have used a similar product to yours for years without any major issue. Imagine as well that the new product you are proposing might improve their life, but not significantly. Plus, you are a newcomer to the market and nobody has ever heard of you in Europe.

In that case, the cost to switch to your product will be quite high and will be measured in terms of risk. The perceived risk for your prospective European client is high, and there is no major incentive for them to change. Your product or solution does not have a track record in their industry in their country, so it represents a risk. In that case, even if your product is interesting, they usually won't switch.

In the case of high perceived risk and low incentive to change, what do you do? You focus on the barrier that you have to overcome and work meticulously to do so. You adjust your approach.

Let's take another scenario: you are trying to target the automotive industry. You produce a new technology that significantly reduces vehicle emissions. As it happens, a new European regulation is about to be enforced for vehicles to reduce CO_2 emissions even further. Imagine that on top of this, a new scandal has just come out and an automotive firm has been accused of cheating while reporting their CO_2 emissions measurements. Clearly, in this context when you target any automotive manufacturer you will get their attention. They have an urgency to act and to make sure they are prepared to comply with this new regulation.

Common perceptions and how to overcome them

Let's go through some very common perceptions that potential European customers express when buying a new product from a new player in the market. And I will also share with you some common strategies to overcome these barriers and win the deal.

Common perceptions that European customers express when buying from a new player

Perception	Solution	Counteract	
1. No budget available for a new purchase	Collect financial data	Build business case	**Cost of not changing** **Return of Investment**
2. New means risk	Reinforce credibility	Build credentials	**Referees** **Case studies** **Introduction to current clients:** face-to-face visits, phone calls **Company history:** experience of management team, government endorsement, certifications
3. It's hard to change	Facilitate a smooth change	Organise change	**Contractual change:** include it in the deal, take over the administrative process **Physical change / migration:** include the physical move or migration in a service proposal or in the deal **Change of habit:** provide training, showcase benefits, do it with them, offer a support line
4. Dealing with a small business means risk	De-risk dealing with your business	Outweigh risk	**Partner with a distributor** **Build your credentials:** referees, case studies, introduction to current clients **Showcase your agility** as a small business
5. If the product comes from overseas I won't have support	Break this perception	Organise support	**Provide support through a local partner** **Plan a local hire for support**
6. There is no major value add from your product in comparison to others	Clarify the perception	Fact finding	**Follow the questioning structure in the flowchart on page 52.**

Let's have a look at these perceptions in more detail, and how to overcome them.

Perception 1: No budget available for a new purchase

I have to admit, sometimes this is *not* a perception. It is real. There is no budget available for a new investment. So, you need to find a way to justify this unplanned cost. Actually, if you have a motivated buyer in front of you, they will usually explain to you what they need to make the purchase happen.

The most effective method is to present a business case for it. You may be able to highlight over a period of one to three years the breakeven and the return on investment. In some cases, it might even be sooner.

To make it easy, lay out two scenarios, as follows …

Scenario one

Scenario one outlines what happens if your prospective client *does not* purchase. This is the default scenario; doing nothing, things stay as they are.

In this scenario, think about the total cost of running the current solution they have. This may include running costs such as maintenance costs, upgrade costs and servicing costs. You may also highlight how many people are involved in running the current solution and their wages. Don't forget to collect as much data as you can about their current costs to be able to show a realistic situation.

If doing nothing exposes the client to a potential risk, you may want to indicate the cost of this risk happening. For example, in the medical sector, if your solution provides better patient management and reduces the cost of medical errors, you may add into this scenario the potential cost of being sued in case of medical error. Another way to look at it is through insurance costs. They would presumably have higher insurance costs than with the patient management system in place.

Scenario two

In scenario two, you highlight what it would look like to *have your solution in place*. You will have to include the costs of migrating to your solution, the training costs and the installation costs.

Then, if you anticipate an increase in revenue or some savings kicking in after a period of time, make sure the period of comparison between scenario one and two gives you enough time to show that. Your client may, for example, be able to sell an extra service, or increase its price point. In terms of savings, your solution may allow a decrease in running costs. In some instance, your solution would remove a risk and therefore decrease insurance policy costs. It's worth adding all of that in.

When I worked for **IBM**, we used to sell very large servers, and our clients would finance these machines. So we would present scenario one with the current monthly instalment and the current maintenance fee of the existing machine. Scenario two would include the new leasing fee, the buyout of the old machine, and the new – lower – maintenance costs. We would always manage to show an increase in capacity and scalability for the same costs. And we would always want to demonstrate that the cost of doing the purchase now was lower than doing it later. (Using leasing is a very good way to get a client to afford a very large investment. The monthly instalments are then part of their running costs.)

While doing this exercise, it's always interesting to show when the breakeven will be.

Perception 2: New means risk

This is a major barrier, and this is a frequent one when you enter a new market: the perception that buying something new and from an unknown player in the market is risky. A buyer's worst fear is to have fingers pointed at them if things go wrong. They fear being accused of not having assessed the credentials of a potential supplier well enough.

To counteract this issue, you have to show your credentials in that industry to reassure your prospective European customers.

They need to feel that others in their industry have used your business without any issues, and that they are happy about it. It will reduce the level of perceived risk in the eyes of your future European customers.

With one of my Australian clients, we used case studies for that purpose. My client developed a series of case studies based on their Australian clients that were from industries we were targeting in Europe. It really helped. This way, European clients thought it was low risk to them to try this Australian product. If large Australian companies in their industry adopted this product on a large scale then it had to be worthwhile and reputable.

It's also very powerful to propose to your prospective European clients introducing them to some of their peers in other countries. A few years ago, we were targeting the large public French railway operator. And we were trying to sell to them new software for their train drivers. I used some of my personal contacts to get my client in front of the right decision maker, and this saved them months of searching for the right person.

But even with a warm introduction, the decision maker still was not fully convinced. Our client already had quite a good customer base in the UK, so we proposed that the French client visit customer sites in the UK that were already using the software. That really helped to get the deal. The level of perceived risk became negligible.

By showcasing your credentials you can reassure your prospective clients.

Perception 3: It's hard to change

This perception might occur due to an actual difficulty implementing a new solution.

Contractual change

For example, you may have been called by an electricity provider recently. In their pitch, some of them offer to organise the transfer of your service for you without you having to contact your current energy provider. It's very smart; they are trying to minimise the administrative hassle caused by switching to a new electricity pro-vider. They are making it easy for you to change.

So imagine in your case how you can smooth the way for your prospective customers to stop buying from their current supplier and buy your product. What barriers can you remove?

When I worked for IBM, they had a finance division. I used to sell servers worth several million euros at the time. So when it was time to change or upgrade, we would estimate the value of the machine currently in use. If it was leased, we would check what the buyout would be. And that allowed us to build the deal: New machine value – Current machine value = Amount to finance. And in that financing we would plan the exit for the next deal.

What solutions can your business come up with?

Migration

In the information technology sector, this perception can be real. Imagine a hospital wanting to buy new software for the manage-ment of patient records. The head of the hospital's worst nightmare would be that something goes wrong, like losing patient data. So, of course you are going to have to make the switch as safe and easy as possible. You clearly have to showcase how easy it will be to migrate to your system. You will also put the emphasis on your experience in successful, secure and zero-downtime migration.

Get inspired by the IT industry, and include the cost of migra-tion for your customer. Make it simple for them.

Physical change and changing habits

One of our clients builds large production lines. When they find a client that's interested in their lines, they need to first visit and assess the factory. A big consideration for them is the physical space required for their equipment. It will dictate the size of the production line they build. They might even have to dig into the ground to fit their machinery in. This means there will be a cost to adapt the client's premises which will need to be taken into account in the total cost of the purchase.

Another aspect is they will have to train the operators on the new line. It will be a whole set of new operations for the company, so it requires training and being able to assist during the initial phases. It is critical to their success that the operators adopt the new line and are happy about it.

You must have a change-management strategy in place and offer to either help the client with the changeover or actually deliver it as part of your solution. You can include a service to manage the physical change (a move, or collecting an old machine). You can also include training for the end-users for them to adopt your product without problems or reluctance.

Perception 4: Dealing with a small business means risk

This leads me to another very common perception you may face if you are a small or a medium-sized business.

This is a challenge that my clients from the healthcare industry often relate to me. They have excellent e-Health solutions and their target market is hospitals, quite often public ones. They regularly go up against the perception that dealing with a smaller player generates risk. The buyer fears if something goes wrong, she will be blamed. It's true that public organisations tend to go for the safe choice, and for this reason they tend to pick the largest supplier. I have seen that happen very frequently.

In that case, you need to play to your strength: because you are a small business, you are agile. The agility of a small business is what large organisations are interested in. How many times have very large multinationals gone over budget and not delivered on time? It's quite frequent.

A small business can't afford to be inefficient. It's easy for a small business to demonstrate how it will adapt to unforeseen circumstances. That won't be the case with a very large organisation. Large multinationals are slow to move and to adapt. They are not as innovative as one would think. Large corporations deal with small businesses because they are looking for innovation. This is the message you can convey as a small to medium-sized innovative business.

The other way to overcome this perception is to partner.

I recommend using existing distribution networks in Europe. One of the advantages of having a local channel partner is that it overcomes the perception your business is too small to deal with a large corporation.

If their current supplier is a distributor of your product, then your issue is solved. In fact, this is really the way to go. For one of my clients, our main target market is large multinationals and we make sure their products are sold by distributors that currently sell to these large multinationals. And it works very well. (In chapter 4 I will go through sales channels in detail.)

Perception 5: If the product comes from overseas I won't have support

This is another perception that European clients express to us when we sell Australian products to them. They really want to be reassured that they will have local technical support.

First of all, as you have seen in chapter 1 about products, there are many ways to organise local support. You can provide technical support through a local partner. They can do the level one support. This means they take the first call and do all the preliminary checks on your behalf before they submit a case to you.

Whatever system you find, you need to have a plan in mind that can be easily implemented. You don't need to go over the top from day one, but you must be ready to quickly implement your plan as your sales grow. For example, as we were approaching a large European manufacturer for one of our clients, they asked us if we could have a technician come in within 24 hours in case of any technical issue. As we were only at the initial stages of the commercial discussion, my client made the commitment to hire a local technician if a deal was signed with them. This commitment came from the CEO of the company, and it is something that will be implemented down the track. It was enough to reassure the client.

Perception 6: There is no major value add from your product in comparison to others

If a client doesn't see a major value add in switching to your product, this should trigger you to conduct more fact finding. Maybe in their mind your product is not so different from the competition and therefore it's not worth changing. If this is what European clients are telling you then you need to fully understand what it means. You have to take a big plunge into what your prospective customers perceive as value.

To overcome this perception, you need to take a step back. I will now take you through a simple process for you to drill down and understand what's really going on. Below I have summarised the approach for you to refer back to at any time.

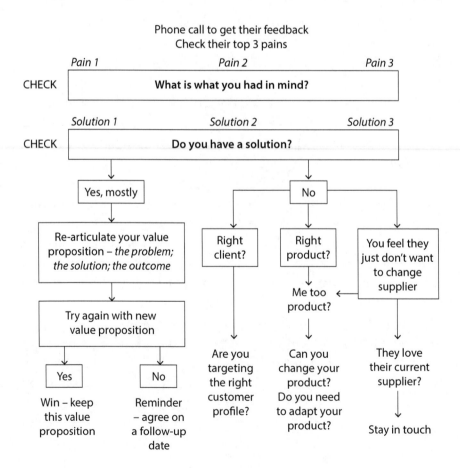

Have your value proposition worked out and clear in your mind before you make the call. (Refer to earlier in the chapter: the problem, the solution, the outcome.)

The first step is to remember that bringing value in your clients' eyes means – most of the time – curing their pain.

Schedule a call

You start the process by scheduling a phone call or a meeting with a customer who decided not to buy your product. You tell them you would like to ask for some feedback about your solution. The way you present it to your lost customer is to tell them you understand that your product does not seem to respond to their needs. You are engaging in a continuous improvement process, and you would like to take their feedback into account in that process. You very much value their opinion.

It may sound like a big ask – but actually, it's not! People love to share their opinion. At Exportia we do that all the time. It is a great way to transform a conversation. In this type of conversation your potential client will be quite open to talk, because you are removing the pressure on her to buy. You are only asking for her valuable thoughts.

Back to the three major customer pains

When you do your call you start with the most important thing: the customer pain. You go back to that point. What is their current preoccupation? What keeps them awake at night? Ask them for their top three problems. Dig into these and ask them why these issues are important. Also ask what impact this has on their business, and which issue is the most important to them. Assess the level of urgency to solve each of these problems.

Are you aligned?

Then you need to check if these three problems are the ones you had identified before. Ask yourself if there is anything you missed. Compare it with the value proposition you had initially prepared the first time you contacted them.

Check now if the solutions you offered initially respond to these three problems.

If your response is mostly yes, then your message did not go across well

It means it may just be a question of you working on the communication of your value proposition again. You understood their problem, and you had a solution for it, but your message was not clear. So now you can articulate your value proposition to them again while you have them on the phone.

With this re-articulated value proposition, are they interested?

If yes, you win! You can keep this new value proposition and re-use it with other customers.

If the customer is interested but not now, you can agree on a time for you to follow up. Use reminders in your customer relationship management (CRM) system or just in your calendar to follow up.

If the client is still not interested, even with a value proposition that has been adjusted to her needs, you need to investigate more. It might be that she has close ties with the competition or your competitor better met her requirements.

If you now understand the most urgent and important problems and you realise your product does not solve these, here's what to do next …

Firstly, you now need to ask yourself if you are targeting the right clients. Are they really your low-hanging fruit? Or is there a different client profile that would feel more interested in your product?

Secondly, do you think you can change anything in your product so it would better fit the bill? Have a discussion with your product development team. Share the customer's pains with your team and ask if you can solve them.

Thirdly, they still don't feel they should buy your product because your differentiators are not significant enough for them to do so. You need to look at a few things and ask yourself and your client a few questions:

- You need to have a true understanding of what the issue really is. Evaluate if your product has in fact little differentiation from the competition. If this is your customer's perception then you need to go back to your competition matrix (see chapter 1) and update your competitive review.

- You need to have another go at finding the customer pain. In what your competitors offer, what does the client find the most important and what problem does it solve for your client? If you really can't solve your customer's problem, or your competitors do a better job, go back to: are you targeting the right customers? Do you need to improve or change your product offering?

Then there is an element that is out of your control: the relationship your prospective client has with their current suppliers. Sometimes, these relationships are so strong and important that you won't be able to make them buy from you instantly. It will take a while. There can be several explanations: it can be common strategic interest, proximity, or a personal relationship with the business owner.

I have one example that comes to mind; I came across a French company that converts automotive vehicles into ambulances and other commercial vehicles – let's call it a converter. They are the first manufacturer of that kind in the French market. Their first supplier is the actual car manufacturer. And this car manufacturer has its factory strategically located near this converter factory. This strategic location provides transport savings to the converter. So any other car manufacturer wanting to work with the converter will battle that existing relationship and the proximity.

You should never give up though. Things can change; the best you can do is to stay around. Relationships may change when people change jobs. And a client that is not happy with her supplier will always change, and when this time comes, be ready to take this opportunity.

Make the first purchase an easy decision

You now have found your prospective customers' top three pains, and you have formulated a value proposition. Your product positioning responds well to their pain. You have also evaluated what the cost of switching to your product is. You have worked on lowering this cost of switching to make it smooth for your potential customer to buy from you. *Now is the time for them to buy!*

There is a simple way to secure the client: make their first purchase a low-commitment and low-risk one. Make their first step working with you a small one.

What we often offer is a trial product. It can also be a 'proof of concept' offer or a 'try and buy' offer. The objective of these first offers is to demonstrate that your product is perfect for your client. It's also an opportunity for you to show that your product delivers on its promises.

The proof of concept offer

Let's take the example of a proof of concept (POC) in the information technology sector. Let's imagine you are a developer of software for hospitals. Your proof of concept will take place with a limited sample of patient records and the application will be used only in one department. The proof of concept will take place over three months. You establish key performance indicators (KPIs) at the beginning of the POC. The KPIs could be:

- zero loss of data

- workers' level of satisfaction with the tool

- zero incidents.

You formalise this at the start of the proof of concept. This way, if your solution meets the KPIs at the end of the three months, the contract is already signed. And you can invoice straight away once it has been demonstrated that the KPIs are met. It's great to finalise the contractual arrangement at the start, so you need to be able to anticipate any issues that could be raised by your contract as early as possible. There is no point investing time and resources for both parties if there are major disagreements on the legal side of things.

The POC is the most comprehensive way to make your client try your product, and to reassure her that the solution is actually going to deliver. As I said, it's common in the IT sector, and in manufacturing it can also be a good way to prove the performance of your machinery. This is often used for solutions that have an impact on a core business process; for example, patient record management in a hospital or a manufacturing line in a factory.

If this approach seems too complex, you can adopt a simpler approach: the 'try and buy'.

The try and buy offer

Companies we have worked with in different sectors have organised different ways for us to get European prospects to try their product. Over the years we have helped our clients to formalise several types of offers. There is the straight 'free sample' offer. One of my clients has made the conscious decision to allocate a budget to free samples. They have an excellent quality product, which in the hands of the right technical person can really speak for itself. So the CEO has agreed to give away samples.

It has worked to some extent; we won over customers because they clearly saw that the product is excellent. On the other hand, there were customers who parked the free sample and we found it really hard to get them to even try it.

What I have learnt about free samples is that they must be linked to a commitment from the customer to test by a specific date and to provide feedback. One day I was doing sales visits with one of my client's distributor's sales representatives in the north of France. And the sales representative I was doing sales calls with had organised her own trial system. She would bring the device to the customer's site, and she would have trained them prior to the trial. On the day, she would drop off the products to test. She would get them to sign a very simple form outlining the products that were lent to them, and the duration of the trial (which would be a week). She would also leave a feedback form which she would later collect. It worked very well; the test had a timeline and a commitment from the client to provide feedback. It was totally a win–win.

To be honest with you, I'm not a big fan of giving away free things. I will always push for a small purchase to start with. It really tests if the client is ready to buy. It conveys the message that the product is of high value, and is perceived as such by the potential buyer.

As we were working on growing the footprint of one of our clients across Europe, scaling to multiple countries, it became quite hard to manage a large fleet of free trial devices. It also became costly. So my client decided to package trial kits, whereby the client would pay for the high-value device but would get the consumables and accessories for free. It worked out very well. It was a great way to test the interest of customers, and prospective customers accepted this system very well.

Following is an example of a form you can include with a trial offer. Feel free to copy it. You can customise it for your own purpose. I would advise you to provide the forms in the local language. It would be good to allow the people testing to express their feedback in their own language – they will share their views more easily and you will get more honest feedback.

Example trial offer form

Customer name:	
Address:	
Contact person:	
Phone:	
E-mail:	
Trial description:	
Duration of trial:	
List of products:	
Start date:	
End date:	

I hereby acknowledge I am participating in a trial as described above.
I commit to either buy the goods at the end of the trial or to return them.

I commit to providing formal feedback at the end of the trial.

Signature:	Date:
Position:	

How to make it with European multinationals

An important part of our work at Exportia is to help our clients work with large multinationals. Our clients are mostly small to medium-sized businesses. We have developed a good track record in securing large deals with European multinationals. Europe is the home of several very large firms: Airbus, Thales, Sanofi, Unilever, Nestlé, Danone, L'Oréal and Shell, just to name a few.

All of the above applies

Many of the tools we have used to gain our clients work with multi-nationals are just as we have looked at so far. It's about positioning your business as a credible brand. You need to overcome any negative perception or concern that the buyer from a multinational could express, as explained in the previous chapter. As indicated earlier, you also want to lower as much as possible the cost of switching to your product, and provide the option for them to buy at a low risk and low price point through a trial period.

Have your positioning ready

What is your value proposition to them? What problem are you solving in this specific industry? How big is the problem? Is it recognised by the industry as a problem? You need to check that your positioning resonates with the targeted multinational. When we approached the French railway operator SNCF on behalf of an energy efficiency software provider, we talked to them about energy savings. I had some insider information that it was one of the top priorities at a high level in the company, so I had my way in. You also need to check how you are comparing to other providers in terms of performance, price, customer service and aftersales support. The bottom line is: it's all about what's in it for them! It's not about what you offer.

Find a common connection with them

When I approach a large multinational on behalf of one of my clients I, of course, look at my network first. Do I know anybody working there in Europe or in Australia? Can they recommend a contact for us? Many people use LinkedIn to get in touch with new contacts. My experience is that this usually fails if you don't have anybody recommending you to that person. I value my network a lot; I'm genuinely interested in what people do. It means that when it comes to approaching someone and asking them for a warm recommendation, I am comfortable in asking for an introduction – it does not come out of the blue.

You have just one shot

I am quite straightforward when it comes to approaching someone in a large multinational. I tell that person precisely what I'm after. I also make it easy for them to forward my request to someone else if required. All the information is provided in a compact e-mail with a brochure attached. I also prepare it in the appropriate language; this can make it easier. Don't assume English suits all Europeans. Your approach, of course, should be professional, responsive and polished – amateurism is banned!

Treat negative answers with care

If you get a negative answer, still acknowledge the reply and thank the person for their time. You can also kindly ask the person for some feedback. I find that people are generally quite helpful. An important point is to ask if you may reach out to them again at a later stage if you find something that is more relevant to them. You may also ask them for the authorisation to reach out if you ever need their expert advice. Interestingly, when it comes to innovative solutions, generally speaking people want to stay on top of the latest innovations in their market, so they like to be informed of any innovation coming out and they agree to stay in touch.

Develop your key account strategy

Once you have validated an initial interest from a multinational, you need to establish a strategy to handle that account. In some cases, you won't be able to sell directly to that European multinational. You need to map out their decision-making process, the stakeholders and their job role, as well as the suppliers they are using for your specific product or solution. For example, large European multinationals usually have up to three preferred distributors to source things such as industrial tools or safety equipment. How can you work with these suppliers or distributors? Again, your positioning is important, as you will need to use it when approaching that supplier. Use the interest of this multinational as your trading value with the distributor to get in the door.

Implement and persist

I know it sounds dumb, but *implementing* the strategy is key. This is the hard part because we can all strategise in our boardroom, but only great implementation pays off. Your mapping is done, your positioning is right, now you need to roll it out. You need to actually get in this supply chain.

You must select the right partner; they need to be aligned with your objectives. You should only select and work with distributors that are actively working and developing their relationships with large multinationals you are interested in. To get them interested, they need to see how you can fit in their range. Study their current range thoroughly and consider how you'd fit in.

Use your sales channels to work with multinationals

If you are targeting multinationals and get their interest, you may still find it hard to sell directly to them. In that case, a distributor already supplying to multinationals will be very interested to work with you to get the deal signed.

Your ability to create interest among large multinationals will make you rise to the top on the distributor's priority list. And this is what you want. Also, keep checking in with these large accounts while working with a distribution partner. You need to make sure they are well looked after. The value of a good channel partner is that it will multiply your reach, ensuring you can not only reach one multinational but dozens of them.

Multinationals often buy through tenders

Partners are great if your product area requires you to respond to tenders. This is the case with many multinationals and government bodies. They often issue tenders for an entire suite of products. They prefer to buy from a single supplier that can provide a whole range of products, rather than buying single products from a large number of suppliers. From the perspective of a large multinational, they like to rationalise their number of suppliers. It's more cost effective for them. It also gives them more bargaining power with suppliers that have a good amount of turnover with them.

Typically, a channel partner or distributor can supply a comprehensive range of products to a multinational. And your product can be part of that range. With most of our clients, which are small and medium-sized businesses, we often work with distributors to secure the sales. And this also sometimes happens once we have done the sales at the end-user level. In the case of one client of ours – who produced a respiratory protection device – we target large accounts and we lobby them to adopt this device. However, when it comes to actually responding to a tender, our distributors do this, sometimes several of them. In this way we make sure that the channel to the product is easily accessible to the multinational.

De-risking big contracts

We love to secure large deals with multinationals. It can really grow sales for our clients in a big way with just one deal. Securing these sales is also a great leveraging tool in the market. You attract new opportunities, you become more visible to future high-calibre salespeople. Your business becomes more attractive for investors, and distributors find your product interesting because their large clients want it.

On the other hand, as you scale up you need to quickly increase your number of very large clients so that you don't rely on one single deal, to de-risk your sales. Really large deals are great, but you need to quickly make sure this client does not represent too large a share of your sales.

Another thing that can be tricky with large multinationals is their requirement for information about your business. Their purchasing department will want to have an idea of the solidity of your business as a supplier. This will especially be the case when the component you sell to them is an important part to their product. They will want to have as much financial data as possible. And if you are a small or medium-sized business that is privately owned, you might not want to do that. Do not be afraid to push back. You can share only the information you want to. Usually this is accepted. However, don't hesitate to showcase your credibility, such as your quality systems, your certifications, and any government funding you have received. Don't make it a sales pitch, but factual.

Make the most of multinationals' incubator or partnership programs

It's interesting to observe the trend of incubators founded and hosted by multinationals. Increasingly multinationals are interested in partnering with start-ups to benefit from their innovation and as a way to give back to the community.

European multinationals have created programs in which they partner either with start-ups or with small and medium-sized enterprises. The programs can take the form of an incubator or it can be an investment fund, or both. For example, Suez has an investment fund focused on waste and water management. Each Suez local entity has a contact person to spot potential applicants for the program. Bayer offers a network of incubators worldwide and is focused on start-ups in life science.

We introduced one of our clients to one such program. The program gave him great credibility and exposure for his business.

He now has sold to one of the Big Four accounting and consulting firms.[1]

If you are targeting a particular European multinational and you think they could benefit from your innovation to improve their internal processes or offer your solution to their clients then it's worth investigating if they have such a program.

Nurturing your newly acquired clients

Finding 'anchor clients'

Securing sales is the key to your success. When we secure a major contract with a large European corporate, we make sure this customer is a reference point for us to further grow the business for our Australian companies in Europe.

We like to secure deals with multinationals that have multiple footprints in Europe. These first deals in the European market are often critical, because you can leverage them with other clients in the same industry. Having a reference customer in Europe places you on the map. It gives you the credibility you need to further expand in Europe.

Recently, we worked on a project for a cloud-based solution. Our client had wonderful references in Asia and in the US, but we quickly realised we needed to secure a first European customer to trigger the attention of potential partners.

Over the last 13 years, we have seen that happening over and over: as soon as we secure the first European customer, things change and doors start to open. It becomes easier to secure distribution partners and it's also easier to sign up additional customers.

This first customer is what I call your 'anchor client'. It's an anchor because it grounds you in the market. We often find that these customers are enthusiastic about your product. They also like to be showcased as the first to adopt a new product.

With one of my clients, when we started in the French market, the turning point was when we secured a large construction

---

1   KPMG, Deloitte, E&Y and PWC.

company as a customer. This customer has been instrumental in the success of our client. He became an advocate for the technology. Working for a large French multinational, he was involved in the major steering committees in his industry; he also had direct connections with regulatory authorities. His involvement provided exposure to other companies in this industry. We also were introduced to French regulatory bodies. It was much easier for us to gain recognition for the Australian technology with this help.

The same thing happened for that customer again in Germany with another multinational in the same sector. Again, the German client recommended the Australian technology to his peers. He was involved in the German industry association. Because he did a thorough trial period of the technology, has was confident he could recommend it. The Australian technology ended up being showcased in one of the official industry publications. Our distributor locally gained the leverage he needed to pursue the entire industry.

These French and German customers were ready to raise the flag for our Australian client because they had taken the product through a validation process. We assisted them in that process with training and ongoing support. They were our number one priority. We did not hesitate to troubleshoot any issue they had on site. We would then regularly check in to see if everything was solved. This level of support gave them trust in the product, so they were confident promoting it to their peers. This is why these two clients became anchor clients.

Customer care: how will you service your European customers?

Nurturing and supporting European customers and leads can sometimes be overlooked by small and medium-sized businesses entering Europe. It can be because inbound enquiries are not looked after – they get lost. An important European customer calls and nobody is aware of the importance of that request. It's hard to qualify the enquiry when you are not familiar with the company name.

In the last 13 years working with small and particularly medium-sized businesses I have noticed that, when exporting is new to the business culture, people in the company tend to keep minding their daily business. They feel they don't have to be involved in that new part of the business. It's often simply because they have not been engaged in the process. They have not been assigned a role in it.

It's often easy to fix. The importance of European client enquiries just needs to be communicated to the team and key people must be well informed and in charge. Once key people understand what's going on and a simple process is established it usually runs smoothly.

Interestingly, businesses at the smaller end of the scale are usually doing a great job – they usually jump on these enquiries. Smaller businesses are used to doing a bit of everything, so it's not unusual for them to respond to new enquiries swiftly. Medium-sized businesses have more staff and so need to clearly outline a process to service these new European enquiries. I recently came across a large business that had a person working from home after hours just to look after these enquiries. This was a great move.

At Exportia, when we on-board a client to provide multilingual European customer service, we define the process we need to follow to handle an enquiry. It is really simple. The most crucial aspect is to determine who in the business has what information – commercial and technical. And we also must establish the qualification process for a lead.

Leads and customer management: the power of a good system

When you start to generate leads in Europe, you need to start recording your activities and the contact details of your leads. For some of my clients, we constantly generate 100 to 200 leads per trade show, we do two or three shows per year, and we get at minimum of one or two enquiries per week. Imagine the amount of contacts that would amount to at the end of the year.

It's particularly important when you have a sales team spread across several parts of the globe. You will need to ensure you have a clear view on the pipeline of opportunities, and at the same time enable your team to collaborate on these opportunities. A spreadsheet, even accessible online, simply won't do the trick. You need something built especially for this purpose. To manage your customer relationships, you need a good system. What's crucial is to make sure each enquiry has been dealt with appropriately. And you must be able to manage leads through your sales process.

At Exportia, we often start with spreadsheets for the initial stages, but then as the number of contacts increases we find we need to have a better system to be productive and make sure we don't lose any information.

There are dozens of good customer relationship management (CRM) systems in the market. I have used many of them over my 20 years of being a sales representative. Frankly, simpler is better!

When I started my business, I was fresh out of IBM. In the IBM style, I implemented the top of the range CRM system, a major brand. But I found it bulky and expensive, and it was an effort to integrate newsletters and social media. I finally decided to move away from it. I implemented a simpler CRM system instead that easily integrated the marketing functionalities I needed. It was a major improvement.

When choosing a CRM system, keep two things in mind:

- How user friendly is it?

- What is the process and cost of integrating new modules?

Complying with the European Union General Data Protection Regulations

The European Union General Data Protection Regulations (GDPR) are the European privacy regulations. They came into force on 31 May 2018. If you offer your products or services to a European resident, even if your business is not registered in Europe, these rules apply to your business if you are processing personal data.

Here are a few issues that you must be aware of:

- Even if you don't make a sale, you are still required to comply.

- As long as it relates to an individual or makes someone identifiable, such as an e-mail address, there is no distinction between personal and business data.

- The safest way to go about being compliant is to ask prospective clients and customers to provide their consent to record their data and to indicate the reason for collecting the information. You can't use this information for anything else other than the reasons you have specified.

- You need to keep a record of that consent, and you need to be able to provide access to their personal data. You should not keep any data that you don't need.

- You need to have a legitimate interest in having this data; for example, somebody has opted in and wants to purchase your product.

- You need to clearly outline in your privacy policy what you are doing with the data.

At Exportia we love to generate leads at trade shows, and we clearly ask for consent from people at the time of collecting their information. We specifically ask them if we can subscribe them to our newsletter, or if we can only send them the information they have requested.

I would advise you to get comprehensive advice on how you can comply with GDPR.[1]

---

1 Exportia and Innovo Legal, Christelle Santelli, conducted a webinar to outline the main obligations under GDPR. https://www.exportia.com.au/video-gallery/

Checklist and templates you can prepare to set you up

Define your ideal customer profile	
Write a case study with existing customers	
Organise your technical support	
Formalise a trial registration and/or a feedback form	
Target an anchor client in the European country you are focusing on	
Define your process to service European customer enquiries	
Establish a system for your customer relationship management	

3 | COUNTRY

Insider's tips for doing business in the European market

This is going to be a fun chapter. I'm so excited to share the insider's tips for doing business in the European market. The goal is for you to get a handle on several things to allow you as a businessperson to be better prepared to succeed at business in Europe and to avoid pitfalls.

What I found out when dealing with non-Europeans in Europe for the last 13 years – and even before when working for IBM in Paris – is that there are errors you can easily avoid by being aware of a few characteristics of Europeans. Typical mistakes that non-Europeans make in Europe often start with **entering too many different countries at once**. It is a very intensive task to enter numerous countries at once, and you can spend a lot of time trying to figure out the market dynamics in many countries at a time. Small businesses have constraints in terms of resources. It's rare to spread your resources thinly and do well in many different countries at a time.

The other typical mistake is to start in a European country **without having gone through a selection process**. I often see Australian companies starting with the United Kingdom because they feel close to this country culturally. However, this country might not be the right one for them or their product. It might be saturated, or just not have the right industry landscape to generate enough demand.

In this chapter, I'm going to focus on key facts that are important to exporters coming from countries outside the European zone. I'm going to make this section very practical.

I will avoid the clichés about the Germans being organised, the French being *this* and the Dutch being *that*. You can read plenty of those in tourist guides. I am rather going to focus on key pieces of information that are often overlooked by non-Europeans and are important when you enter the European market.

As a French-born person and having lived and worked in different parts of Europe, I will draw on my experience in decoding and explaining to my Australian clients how and why these Europeans are different!

What makes Europe different?

Europe, an ensemble of countries

If you compare Europe to the US, the US would seem to be a large homogeneous block – Europe is not! Europe is a multitude of countries that are diverse, have different economic situations, varied cultures, and speak different languages. Yet, they share the same land mass and are interlinked in their economies, flow of populations and social structures.

When entering the European market, non-European companies often expect Europe to be like a unified block. It is not. In my experience, when taking non-European businesses to Europe, I tend to take this diversity as an interesting way to approach the market. It is easier to have an impact and create some traction in a smaller economy. You will see the effects of your work quickly.

Then you will be able to make the most of the natural linkages between European countries and leverage them. If you succeed in Germany, for example, you will be able to use your German success, customer experiences and track record to make inroads in other European countries. It will have a great impact. Your German-speaking customers will be able to be referees for other potential customers, from Austria and Switzerland, who also speak German. It's easily done. Your French-speaking referees can talk to French, Swiss and Belgian customers.

At Exportia, we often look at the European customers we deal with and check their footprint in other European countries. That helps us expand our customers' presence. We ask them to make some warm introductions to their colleagues in other countries. That is an easy way to expand.

The long term versus the short term

Europeans will take notice of your business if you can demonstrate that you are committed to their market for the long term.

My business is based in Australia. Over the years, I have come to realise that my Australian clients often took a very short term view on our development plans for the European market. It did strike me, because I am a European. My short term is their long term. For me, five years is a short-term period, for them it is long term.

That does result in plenty of fun conversations. At the moment, we work in the European safety industry on behalf of one of our clients. In this industry, particularly in Germany, the distributors we deal with often have been in place for the last hundred years. They build 10-year plans and they implement them. For example, they plan particularly well managed transitions. I have seen 5- to 10-year plans when it comes to replacing a top executive. When I explain that to my Australian clients, they find it unreal: 'Who knows what will happen in 10 years!'

Europeans value stability, and many of them will only start taking a business seriously when it has been active in their market for three to five years. Before that, there will be a lot of professionals in your industry who will watch your business's activities and check in from time to time to see if you are still active in their market. Once they are confident you are here to stay, only then will they talk to you. After being in place in a European market for three to five years, a whole new level of opportunities opens up.

Persistence is therefore a key to success in Europe.

It's open for trade

Europe is a place open for trade and open for newcomers. According to the European Union, the EU is the world's biggest trader, accounting for 16.6% of the world's imports and exports.[1]

EU trade: key figures

EU share of world exports and imports:	16.6% – 2014
Foreign direct investment in EU:	€4,583 billion – 2014
EU outbound foreign direct investment:	€5,749 billion – 2014
Manufacturing trade surplus, oil excluded:	about €350 billion – 2013
Services trade surplus:	€163 billion – 2014
EU development aid:	€56.5 billion – 2013

As Europeans, we are used to diversity within our own continent. Our close neighbours speak a different language and have a different culture, and they are often only hundreds of kilometres away.

So, as a non-European you won't be so much different to another European company entering the market. You will just be another one in the room! And this is fine.

European languages – what English speakers don't realise

In the Anglo-Saxon world, there is little exposure to other languages. The supremacy of English does not really encourage teaching other languages to Americans or Australians. Europeans learn English systematically, and sometimes another language.

---

1   *The European Union Explained – Trade.* March 2016, The Publications Office of the European Union. https://publications.europa.eu/en/publication-detail/-/publication/9a2c5c3e-0d03-11e6-ba9a-01aa75ed71a1

A study published by the European Union shows that 60% of lower secondary level pupils studied more than one foreign language in 2014.

Native English speakers who don't speak any foreign languages often think they can get by with English. Most of the time you can. However, your European competitors will have their translations in several languages sorted out. It's quite natural for them to understand that they will not sell to Europeans in English; they will sell to their European customers in their own language. I remember a Swiss distributor of ours being so happy that our Australian product collateral was translated into German – she did not have to ask for it. It created a relationship of trust straight away with the Australian brand.

At Exportia, one of our strengths is that we all are multilingual. We have the capability to train sales teams in French, German, Italian and Spanish. Imagine being told about the technical features of a technology in a language you haven't quite mastered. The person who teaches you has a strong accent that nobody has taught you at school. There are so many accents of English!

How comfortable would you be explaining how this technology works to your clients?

Probably what will happen then is that even just having been just trained, you will avoid selling this new technology, and you will rather sell what you are comfortable with. There are always exceptions. For example, if you deal with very large scale infrastructure projects, your entire project may be managed in English. And English won't be an issue then.

Five areas to watch in the post-Brexit climate

As I write this book, Brexit is now becoming a reality. There is little or no possibility of reversing the decision. Now the modalities of the implementation of Brexit are being discussed. The British Prime Minister is now negotiating with the European Union.

Putting my disappointment aside to see the UK leaving the EU, now is the time to watch how things will evolve. And for me, that means understanding how it will impact our clients in the coming months, or more likely years.

The UK leaving the European Union has a direct impact on trading with Europe for non-European companies. I highlight here five areas that will change in the coming months:

- tax
- intellectual property
- norms and standards
- EU funding
- staff travel.

This is totally a work in progress and needs to be watched month after month. Business is expected to continue as usual until the UK is officially out of the EU. It is expected to happen in early 2020.

Value-added tax and import duties need to be watched

One of the benefits of trading among EU member countries is that you do not pay customs duties in the EU. The EU also has defined import duties for each category of product to be paid when an EU member imports a product from a non-EU member.

It means non-European companies will need to watch what import duties will be applied by the UK once it leaves the EU. It may well be different from the EU in the near future.

Another area to watch will be value-added tax (VAT). Swati Dhingra, Assistant Professor of the London School of Economics, explains it simply: 'Britain would not have access to the coordinated VAT collection of the EU. So a 20% VAT would need to be paid at the UK border, and the importer would no longer have the convenience of combining this with domestic VAT payments.'

These two points will be important to watch in the coming months and years.

Intellectual property protection: one application for the EU and one for the UK?

Non-European companies currently applying to protect their trademark through the Madrid Protocol get to register their trademark in 97 countries with one application. The European Union (EU) is part of the Madrid Protocol. In addition, if you would like to register your trademark in the EU you currently have to lodge an application for your trademark to be valid in the 28 countries of the European Union.

Now if the UK exits the European Union, the question is, in the UK market what will happen to your IP if you have registered it under an EU banner, Europe-wide?

It is clear that current applications will keep covering the UK as part of the EU. When the renewal comes up, or when a new application is lodged, you will need to look again at what the UK has negotiated with the European Union.

European Union norms and standards: what about the CE Mark?

In terms of norms and standards, the European Union has harmonised its standards. It means that, for example, a product which is CE marked does not need in many cases to get additional certification.

But will the UK recognise the CE Mark as a valid standard after Brexit? Hopefully yes, but what happens if not? In that case, the UK would have to create their own set of standards or negotiate with the European Union to use their standards. It would mean that you would have a certification process for the UK and one for the EU.

Two certification processes instead of one? Cost wise, that will have to be taken into account. Let's hope an agreement is found with the EU there as well.

Access to EU funding

Today, I was at one of my Australian clients. They have established a company based in the UK in order to access European Union funding. Now they anticipate having to move their company either to Germany or the Netherlands if they want to keep benefiting from this funding over time. The CEO was telling me she thinks they have no chance of getting an EU grant again if they are based in the UK. It is an unknown at the time of writing, but it may need to be considered if you have a technology that can fit into some of the projects that the EU is funding.

Travel of your staff, hired by your UK company, within the European Union

If you have an established office in the UK and you have staff flying in and out of the UK to do business with the rest of Europe, they will probably have to go through a visa process for business visits. Depending on what the UK is able to negotiate with the EU, it might be a simple process. The minimum expectation is that it should work like other non-EU members, such as for Swiss citizens.

When it comes to posting staff hired by your UK company for several months for projects in the European Union, work permit arrangements will probably change.

Being culturally sensitive

From my 20 years in sales in the European market, I'd like to share with you some of the potential cultural pitfalls. I wish to warn you that some of them might sound politically incorrect. However, they are not. They are just facts. There is not right or wrong in terms of culture. And there is no better or worse either. It's just about the way you deal with it.

One of the best books I've ever read about culture is *Riding the Waves of Culture: Understanding Diversity in Global Business* by Fons Trompenaars. It is an excellent read and is very useful for understanding different communication styles. I also like that Fons Trompenaars is a pure product of cultural diversity with his French and Dutch background.

The book gives you very good general guidance on the differences in communication styles between Europeans. It goes from very direct communication styles with our Nordic and Scandinavian colleagues to a more indirect style with our Southern

Europeans, Italians, Greeks and Spanish. The French are a bit in the middle. So you can imagine that a Swedish colleague giving very direct feedback to an Italian colleague would likely offend her.

The other dimension to the Fons Trompenaars approach is the relationship to the group. According to Trompenaars, you have two opposite ends of the spectrum: the cultures that care more about the group (a family unit, or a team) and the cultures that care more about the individual. So in the management of teams, you need to integrate this in your relationships with Europeans.

Scandinavians are more focused on the individual and Mediterraneans are more group-oriented. It matters in many different situations. If you have some feedback to give to an Italian you want to be careful not to give direct feedback to an individual in front of her peers. You would provide group feedback and then provide personal feedback individually. Or if you come from a group-oriented culture, you should make a point of giving direct feedback to your colleagues from Scandinavia.

One of the mistakes that Australians often make is to set up a team in the UK that is then supposed to grow sales in continental Europe from the UK. I have even seen things like having a British salesperson travelling back and forth from the UK to try to sell to French distributors and travelling with an interpreter. This company had no sales in the UK: it was interested in France and Denmark. The Danes were fine dealing with the British rep and the Australian HQ. But the French, even if they were interested, did not go ahead. When I was appointed to take that role by the CEO, I was very successful at growing the sales, creating trust with the French distributors. It would have taken a non-French speaker many more years to get to a million euros in sales. I had to train more than a hundred distributor sales representatives. You cannot do that in English; the sales teams at the distributors won't be comfortable asking questions and taking you to their customers.

Who manages who?

As you start building your teams in each European country, the question of 'who manages who?' emerges. Recently I was in Paris to exhibit at a conference. As the delegates went back to the amphitheatres, I started to go around and meet my fellow exhibitors. One of them was quite senior and she had held Europe-wide management positions. She was a French national, and we came to talk about the German market. She found that however hard she worked to support the German team, she was never 'German' enough!

Being French, having worked in the German market for 20 years and being fluent in German, I realised that once I had got sales going in this market and wanted to take things to the next level, I would need local help. I started to think what the next steps would be to establish German management. It makes much more sense and things move much faster if you scale activities with a local. But, this is not always practical for a small business new in the European market. First of all, from a budget point of view, small businesses may not be able to afford to hire a senior manager. And as you will see in chapter 6 on team, it is really hard to hire in the German market – the job market is so tight! And as a newcomer in the market, it's sometimes hard to convince someone to switch.

The other way around works though: French team members can easily be managed by German managers. And you can easily find French employees who speak German. It's still common for French schools to teach German. I have always managed to find bilingual French-Germans for my own business and for my clients.

Another example is the British managing the French and the French managing the British. It's usually quite hard to make it work. If you have a British manager managing a French team, make sure they are open-minded and have the cultural awareness to do so. Same for a French manager that has British teams. There is a profound historical rivalry between the two nations that is ingrained. Personally, I don't have these feelings – I am quite impartial. However, this is not the case for everyone. This is where some cultural training might be a real value add if you feel your team does not work well together. There might be a need for better understanding.

As a general rule, it depends on the person and their experience in the country where they are supposed to work, and their personality. For example, I'm French, but it works well for me in Germany because I'm a very structured person. I establish processes with sales teams and abide by them. I usually announce my agenda to my German team members, clients or distributor when I schedule a meeting with them. I would not always do that for a meeting with a French client. The French are more flexible and willing to discuss whatever subject you want to discuss at the meeting. They will work around it.

Small and medium-sized businesses need to have a focused approach in Europe

At Exportia, we always advise focusing on one or two countries only to get started in Europe. The trick is to secure the first sales as quickly as possible and with the smallest amount of investment. The only way a small to medium-sized business can achieve that in Europe is to be focused.

The European Union is a very diverse market, and it means every time you are entering a new country you have to familiarise yourself with the local situation. You will have to translate your brochures and manuals into that language. It's not a huge cost, but if you multiply it by the number of EU languages, it can add up. You would also have to travel to each market. The more countries you travel to, the more time and money it's going to cost.

Being focused is a better way to proceed; you will get a better grasp more quickly and it will be cheaper for you to do so.

Selecting your top European country

Picking the best country in Europe for your product is an essential step. The key is to choose the country that has the best potential and is the hungriest for your product or solution. It's not only about the market size, it is also about the appetite of this country to buy your product in the short term.

Remember, this is about securing your first clients rapidly. A major country such as Germany offers enormous potential given its size, but it's quite risk averse when it comes to adopting new technology, and generally speaking is averse to change. So, the statistics may look good, but it will take you a while to crack that market. How long can you wait?

This is what we are mitigating when we choose the top European countries for a product. We want to pick the countries that are going to be early adopters. Then you will be in a position to scale to other European countries.

At Exportia we guide our customers in this process. In chapter 8 of this book I will show you how to conduct your selection to find your top two countries.

Each European country has a different profile

I have prepared several country profiles with information that I find useful to know for small businesses in the European market. As mentioned earlier, small businesses often make the mistake of rushing into one specific country, without having undertaken a careful selection. These profiles highlight interesting facts, such as the multinationals that originate from this country, the share of SMEs in their economy, and the number of hospitals. You will find these country profiles in appendix A.

4 | SALES CHANNELS

Getting your product to your end-users

What sales channels are and why they are important

Let me get our terminology right to make sure we understand each other. In this section, I cover the subject of distribution channels, also called sales channels and distributors. In the IT industry they are also called channel partners.

These sales channels buy your product or software from you and sell it to their customers. They make a margin from doing so.

Most of our customers at Exportia are small to medium-sized businesses. The Sales Channel Pillar in our methodology is critical to the success of this size of businesses. I don't know one small and medium-sized business that does not carefully watch their resources. Small business owners and their team are time poor and manage their budget carefully. Establishing good sales channels in Europe is the fastest, most cost-effective and lowest risk method to enter the European market. The main reason is simply that you are then not required to establish a subsidiary in Europe to generate revenue.

Often the misconception is that you have to hire locally to get the business started. This is not true. You can generate your first million euros in sales without having a European office or staff.

This chapter about sales channels is one important pillar in generating revenue. My advice is to generate revenue with your distributors first. This way you build your understanding about the market, and you start to identify who's who in the zoo. It will also enable you to start spotting potential future recruits for your business in Europe. When building business for my clients in Europe from the ground up with the local distributors, that is exactly what I do. I keep my eyes open for good salespeople in the field who are already dealing with my target market and have a good reputation.

There are many benefits in building your understanding of the European market with your distributors prior to recruiting your own sales team. First, you will build a more attractive offer for a sales position by having proven that your product is selling in Europe. Thus, you will attract better sales people. Secondly, you will also be a better manager; you will know the market and will be able to better guide them in their job. Thirdly, you will already have a good picture of the market so you will be able to assess the quality of job applicants and what they tell you.

I've heard so many stories from companies that come to us. Some of them had hired a person based in Britain, right at the start of their launch in Europe. That person was quite senior, and of course the salary package was high. It turned out that the French market picked up much more quickly than the British market. So that person would fly back and forth from the UK to France with an interpreter. He did not succeed in turning this strong interest into sales. So, it started to be costly to have this high-salary investment not paying off. Plus, the CEO of the Australian business did not get transparency on what was happening in the French market, so he could not take action.

When the UK-based representative moved on and we were mandated for this project, we focused on working with the French distributors to generate sales, which we did by training their sales team, doing visits to end-users with them, and generating leads.

Of course, for us, what is key is to be able to train sales teams from the distributors in their language. I will describe this process in detail later in this chapter.

While building the first million euros in sales with the French distributors, I also kept my eyes open for people I could potentially recruit to take sales further. I was able to identify a person at a trade show. I could get a feel for that person as a sales rep from the eyes of my distributors and key French end-users. I knew the market inside out, and was able to train that person easily.

It is also valuable to build significant revenue before you hire a local person and create a subsidiary, because of the cost of laying off an employee in Europe. Generally speaking, because of workplace laws it is extremely hard to lay off somebody who does not perform. It is quite costly as well. If you are unfamiliar with the local laws, the back and forth may also cost you time and money. A company we recently started working with told us it cost them 250,000 euros to lay off their general manager in Europe. They were okay because the business already had significant sales, but a smaller business would really have struggled.

Five steps to establishing strong sales channels

Over the past 13 years I have worked with many Australian small businesses involved in high-tech industries, ranging from medical devices, biotechnologies, clean technologies, and ICT to electronics and advanced manufacturing. What always struck me during this period was the challenge for small businesses to generate high levels of sales from their distributors – and, particularly in our case, European distributors. The process would often require a lot of investment in the overseas market to initially get the distributor on board. Then, once they were on board, sales were frequently disappointing.

So I decided that it was the time to stop the debacle, and so developed a simple solution to this ongoing problem. I will now outline a straightforward process which will ensure that your distributors work for you, which in turn will ensure you achieve successful sales results.

The five steps in this solution are:

1. Profile

2. Select

3. Engage

4. Activate

5. Manage.

Step 1: Profile

The first step in this process is profiling your ideal distributor.

Small businesses that are already working with channel partners in the ICT sector would be very familiar with this process. In other industries, business owners need to review their current distributors and identify the ones that have worked well for them previously and why. This exercise will maximise a business owner's chances of recruiting successful distributors. These distributors may be based in your domestic market or overseas; it does not matter which.

Let's get started by identifying three simple characteristics that define the profile of your ideal distributor or channel partner.

Characteristic 1: What type of distributor is right for you?

This is an important point for you to determine in the initial stages of recruiting a distributor to your business. There are different types of distributors – some will be better suited to your business than others. Some distributors are very orientated to *catalogue selling*. They usually sell a very broad range of products, which means it can be hard to attract their attention. On the other hand, the advantage of working with this type of distributor is that they may have a very good footprint in the market.

If your product or solution is more technical (as is the case for many of our clients), you will need a more *solution-selling* type of distribution partner. In this scenario, the sales representatives are more focused on selling a solution that solves a problem rather than a commodity sale.

The next step is to ascertain the profile of sales representatives that are best suited to selling your product.

Characteristic 2: Which clients and end-users should your distributor focus on?

At this point you need to list the target clients you are focusing on for current and future sales. Who will be the final end-users of your product? By constructing an idea in your mind of your ideal distributor's profile you can easily check if a particular distributor is right for you. If a distributor doesn't currently sell to your target markets or industries, don't waste time with them. A critical factor for success is to show them where the low-hanging fruit is for your business. Make it easy for them to be successful and sell quickly for you. Defining this target market is a key criteria for your overall success.

Characteristic 3: Identifying complementary and competing products

If you consider your business's product or solution, you may already be aware if there is an associated ecosystem of complementary products that can be sold in combination with your product or that require the same skillset to sell. For example, one of our clients sells respiratory protection equipment, so we usually try to source distributors that also sell foot protection for them. Then, depending on the brand they sell, you can quickly determine at what price range they are positioning their business. Do they sell cheap commodity products? Or are they able to sell high-end, innovative, premium-priced products?

Another good method is to see if it would be beneficial for you to sell your products via a distributor that already sells products or solution that your competitors sell. From a distributor's perspective, this approach may offer a good alternative if they are attempting to broaden their range. Likewise, your product or service may provide a good competitive differentiator which may allow you to get some market share. Alternatively, you may elect to take the opposite tactic and choose not to work with a distributor who is selling a competing product. However, it's an interesting avenue for you to explore and see if you could benefit from a distributor salesforce that is already used to selling your type of product. It's important to remember that they know the clients and they already have a well-developed sales skillset in your industry.

These three characteristics are a good starting point for you to profile your ideal distributor. For more detail on your ideal distributor profile, you may want to download our online tool from our website (www.exportia.com.au/downloads).

Step 2: Select

Above we looked at profiling your ideal distributor. Now we will be focusing on the process involved in selecting a distributor for your business. Whenever I talk to Australian small business owners, all too often I discover that they just signed up with the first distributor who approached them. They did not take their time and review a range of different distributors and then conduct a selection process.

Let's have a look at how you should make this choice.

Mapping the distribution landscape

This is your first step in determining the best distributor for your business. Having identified the profile of your ideal distributor or partner, you now need to find these operators within the overseas market. One very easy method is to investigate your competitors' distributors or partners' networks in the selected target country. For example, checking out the 'where to buy' section on their website can give you lots of valuable information. Once you have checked your competitors' distribution network, I recommend that you proceed in the same way with companies that have complementary products to yours. It is usually preferable to choose companies that are aligned with your business's positioning.

For example, if you manufacture high-end lawn mowers, check out the distribution network of a high-end rake manufacturer. Trade shows, particularly in Europe, are a very good source of information. Identify the largest trade show in your industry in the country you wish to target, and then review the exhibitor list to identify the key distributors in the market. Generally speaking, the best way to achieve good results is to interview an opinion leader – just humbly ask for their advice. Don't hesitate to reach out; you will be surprised to discover that most people are very happy to share their knowledge when you explain to them clearly what you need to know and why. Assure them that you won't take up too much of their time; you just need a few distributors' names and, ideally, a contact name to get started.

Selecting carefully is key to achieving success with a distributor

All too often, small business owners come to me saying that their distributor did not perform well. And guess what – most of the time it's because they engaged the first distributor that came to them or they did not conduct a thorough selection process. Now that you have established your list of potential distributors, rate them against the selection criteria you defined in your ideal distributor profile. Don't exclude small distributors as they are often able to develop sales much more quickly than a large distributor and are usually easy to work with. They may bring you your first sales.

When you first start narrowing down your list, fill in all of the relevant information on a spreadsheet to compare against your selection criteria.

First approach

When you approach a distributor for the first time, ensure that you have your company profile and your unique selling proposition ready. You may decide to talk to or send an e-mail to the purchasing or product manager or a technical director if appropriate. These people are very time poor so make it easy for them by sending an e-mail that is brief and to the point. At this stage, simply state clearly that you are planning to launch your product into the market and would welcome their feedback. You can then add a short paragraph on your positioning and attach your company profile. The other important point is to let them know that you are intending to go through a distributor selection process. Don't make the mistake of adopting a 'begging' position, even though you are a small business and they may be a huge company. It's just being professional to go through an evaluation process, and the distributor is likely to view that action favourably.

By following these steps you will ensure you are well prepared before you move into the engagement phase of the distribution process.

Step 3: Engage

I will now outline a critical step when working with distributors. This step establishes the basis for either success or failure of your exporting activities since small businesses often don't know how to frame their approach to distributors or partners.

Trading terms

At a very basic level of engagement, you need to ensure that your trading terms are right for you. Let's assume your overseas distributor price list is ready. The things you need to check are that you have clearly stated the Incoterms related to that price, as well as the city and country; for example, 'ex-works (EXW Sydney, Australia)' or 'delivery at place (DAP Munich, Germany)'. If you are not familiar with Incoterms, I recommend that you register for a training session with your local export organisation. Export associations, government organisations and business chambers usually run workshops on this. We also have a webinar recording available on this topic on our website.[1]

Next, you need to make sure your price list includes a validity date and that your payment terms are clearly stated. In chapter 1 about product you will find an example price list.

---

1   https://www.exportia.com.au/video-gallery/trading-terms-webinar/

Distributor prices

When you issue pricing in the European market, be aware that by law price increases need to be announced in writing 90 days prior to the date of the increase. Be prompt with this, otherwise buyers will refuse your increase because they have been informed too late.

Remember I mentioned this point in chapter 1: you cannot impose their selling price on a distributor. They must have the absolute freedom to choose their selling price. It's *illegal* to impose a sell price on them. This is a very sensitive topic, and I would never mention in writing to a distributor that you question their sell price. With one of my clients, we had a major issue with a distributor, a behemoth in the market. This prominent distributor did not position my client's product well in the market – it discounted the product.

We were still in the launch phase of the product. It became a major issue for my client, as this was a premium product. Having a high-value product discounted so heavily discouraged other distributors from taking on the product. But the distributor didn't care. They are a major player. They sell a very large volume of very diversified products. So, when they win a tender they just want to make sure the deal is profitable overall. My client's product was just a drop in the ocean for them. The only option we had was to increase our sell price to them, to minimise their ability to discount.

Payment terms

Depending on the European country you are dealing with, the usually accepted payment terms are 30 to 60 days. I would say the maximum you should accept is '60 days end of month'. I always make a point to push for 30 days when I negotiate terms with a distributor. The reality is all our clients are small businesses. They need to be paid fast. When we start to get large orders from European distributors, we like to get quick payments. It can be risky for our customers to have unpaid large orders going out of their factory.

What works very well initially with distributors, and we usually get it accepted by European distributors, is payment before dispatch. The other option that is greatly appreciated by European distributors is to offer a small discount on early payments: perhaps from 0.5% to 2%, depending on the amount. We usually like to do this for large orders.

Exclusivity

Exporters are often asked for an exclusivity agreement by distributors. I have a strong position on this: no exclusivity is my general rule whenever I negotiate with a distributor. Small businesses need to be able to keep control of their distribution, and granting exclusivity to a distributor means that they won't really have to go the extra mile for you. If you ever do decide to give exclusivity to a distributor, it should be for a limited time only and subject to sales performance. You really need to frame your agreement so that you are in a position to walk away if your distributor is not performing well for you.

How many sales channels?

The number of distributors you should appoint really depends on the size of the target market and distributor. In Europe, for example, I suggest that you initially only appoint one distributor in a small market such as Belgium, and a minimum of two in very large markets such as Germany. Then you can increase these numbers. Make the situation more manageable for yourself by appointing one distributor at a time.

The number of distributors you appoint also depends on your ability to train them. Are you able to train 20 new distributors at once? Or would it be more manageable to start with three?

Negotiating with sales channels

The way to negotiate your terms with a distributor is to start from the best position for your business. For a new distributor, it's fair to provide payment in advance. In the case of my business team, whenever we are dealing with European distributors, we usually stick to 30 days net or end of month. As you may have seen in our price list template, I also like to add the condition: 'We reserve the right to change trading terms in case of late payments'. I urge you to adopt a similar practice.

To make it easy for your overseas distributors, deal in their currency. Of course, for the sake of simplicity, you may want to limit your transactions to a limited number of currencies to start with (euros). In terms of the Incoterms, try to impose ex-works as it will make your life easier. The distributors may already have much better deals in place than you do with freight forwarders, and may be in a better position to negotiate shipping costs. Also, it means you won't have to manage overseas customs and local taxes.

When I start the negotiation process I observe very strict principles. Firstly, I'm not a big discounter, and if I do offer a discount it's usually not very large. Secondly, when a distributor wants to negotiate a term, I usually like to be able to trade it against something. It could be a new product positioning in a catalogue, a marketing campaign, or something similar. Don't always consider price only.

Don't be afraid to walk away if the distributor is trying to push you towards trading terms that don't suit you. It just means they are not right for your business.

Distributor margin

A recurring question of exporters that consult us is: how much margin should I give to a distributor? Once again, you need to be aware of your starting point; it should not be dramatically different to the margin of Australian distributors.

In principle, a margin level should depend on the role undertaken by the distributor. You need to clearly define what role they are going to play for you. For example, are they going to provide aftersales support for you? What marketing campaigns have they committed themselves to running for you? How many sales representatives have been trained in your product?

The next aspect to consider in terms of a distributor's margin is their volume of sales. You need to think about what volume of sales would mean you would be prepared to give them a higher margin.

Distribution agreements

The first question to ask is: should you have one?

Actually, the response is not always a straight yes. Negotiating a distribution agreement sometimes takes a lot of time; six months to a year, depending on the complexity of the contract. We don't usually push for a contract in the first months we work with a distributor. We first like to assess if they are suitable and if they have the appetite to sell now, before we go into a contractual agreement. We have done that on a regular basis. It is usually well accepted.

The second question we often get asked is: should we use our distribution agreement or the distributor's agreement? If you already have one you really want to push to all of your distributors then that's fine. One of our clients made the decision to systematically use their own distribution agreement. In that distribution agreement, there are several clauses they really want distributors to sign on to. Over the years, they have had distributors copy their product. That is why they have a very strong clause in their agreement about intellectual property.

But mainly it depends on the size of your distributor. If you deal with a very large multinational, they will ask you to sign their contract. If this is the case, you can then push to add some clauses that are of particular interest to you; for example, a clause around protection of your intellectual property.

Saying no to disadvantageous clauses

As a small business, you can say no! I guarantee you, you can. It may take a bit of time to get it over the line. And it's not about saying no to everything. It is about accepting what is reasonable, and refusing what you can't comply with as a small business.

Small businesses are often scared to say no to large organisations. The reality is: when you start working with a very large distributor, you are not important to them. At the start, you both will generate little turnover. So the distributor usually accepts this and is usually not rigid if you say no. Down the track, when the sales grow, it will be a different story.

I refuse clauses that can be a threat to the financial wellbeing of the companies we work for. Our clients are mainly based in Australia, and they often ship goods from Australia to Europe. Therefore, they rely on third parties for their prompt deliveries. I don't want them to pay penalty rates because a freight forwarder had some issues; it's too risky.

Should I get a lawyer involved?

Yes, you should get a lawyer involved. Preferably a European lawyer; they can take you through the peculiarities of a specific country.

For example, in France the distributor will ask you if their turnover with you is above a certain threshold. The distributor is not trying to be a pain. In France, chains of supermarkets are very powerful, and sometimes they can represent by far the major client of a small producer. It creates a dependence of the producer towards the supermarket chain. The French regulators have established a rule to protect small producers in that case. That is why the distributor will ask you that.

A local lawyer is best placed to explain such issues.

Penalties

Watch closely for penalties mentioned in the contract. Sometimes it is fine to accept them, because it's related to a process you control. You just need to make sure that the process is known and respected by your team 100% of the time. Make sure your business is not exposed.

Bonuses and discounts

These are usually negotiated on a yearly basis. My general rule around giving away extra discounts and bonuses is to understand what it will bring to your business.

In European distribution agreements, you will often see parts where the distributor details the different tasks they accomplish as a distributor. And in front of each task they ask for a bonus to complete this task. Sometimes it's just a trick to extract more discount from you for just doing their distributor job. That annoys me, and I usually refuse them. But I try to offer alternatives that are attractive to my client in terms of business development and are interesting for a distributor.

Distributors' program

This is the ultimate benefit! Once you have more experience dealing with distributors, you can develop a program for them. You can articulate in that program the different types of distributors (such as tier 1, tier 2, tier 3 ...), their obligations (minimum annual turnover) and their rewards (percentage discount). You can use this channel program as a useful engagement and activation tool.

Step 4: Activate

Activate your distribution in Europe

I personally really enjoy this part of the exporting cycle as this is when you start to achieve some good sales results!

In the initial stages of your exporting operation you may not need a very sophisticated distributor program. Your focus will mainly be on 'hand holding' your distributor and showing them what you require. Remember that they have other products to sell and, naturally, their sales representatives won't be willing to focus on a product that is a hard sell. As a new item in their range, they may feel that it's harder to sell your product than their usual product range.

Training the sales team

This is the first key point: you will need to make the effort to train their sales representatives. You will be able to show them how they can obtain quick wins and where the 'low-hanging fruit' can be found. You have to tell them which industry to focus on as well as what problem your product solves for that industry. Another area you need to be prepared to educate your distributor about is how to present your product or solution to a prospective client (what are the key elements that are going to trigger a prospect's interest?).

Finding champions

Over the years, we've found that having champions on board and looking after them has worked very well for our clients. In the case of very large distributors, it is very hard to get the attention of everyone. There will always be a few distributors' sales representatives who will have a keen interest in your product. These are the ones you want to focus your energy on. They will be willing to push your product forward and demonstrate its benefits to their colleagues. You need to make sure your champions have everything they need in order to be in a good position to sell your product.

Giving them the tools

Sales tools can be as simple as making sure your distributors have access to brochures in their own language and that they know where to find technical information on your website. Case studies work very well; it is very reassuring for a client to hear who else has bought your product and is happy with it. In terms of your champions, you may also want to give them samples or kits so they are able to demonstrate the product.

Generating leads

This is a key consideration to your success – particularly in the B2B space. A distributor or a channel partner is more likely to come on board when they see that their client has requested the product. I know it is frustrating because in an ideal world you would want the distributor to find clients for you – after all, that is why you give them a margin. However, the reality is that generating sales leads for them can get you where you want to be more quickly, as well as ensuring your distributor starts putting in a good effort. It is also useful for you to develop a good relationship with end-users.

Yearly sales and marketing programs

If you are dealing with a large distributor, you may be able to tap into the programs they run. The distributor will often stipulate that to be involved in their sales and marketing program you must be one of their key suppliers or offer them a strategic differentiation. Frequently, these programs are not available for free; instead, they make you pay to attend. You need to know upfront what everything is going to cost to ensure that your margin is kept under control.

A key principle you can adopt when you are starting with a distributor is: you need to give them a realistic sales target. In the beginning, you should make this target easily achievable and then, over time, you will want them to stretch their efforts on your behalf. At this point, you can develop a marketing program with them, such as a common presence at trade shows and/or a specific industry lead-generation plan. You can also ask them to make a commitment on these actions. It's then up to you to give them financial incentives around specific goals, marketing campaigns and sales targets.

Down the track you can build a structured, tiered distributors' program whereby key distributors receive a higher margin and can obtain additional rebates according to specific key performance indicators and sales targets. These details should all be articulated around your strategic sales goals in terms of growth.

It's important to keep this program simple to implement for your distributors and easy for you to track. Be very realistic about this!

Step 5: Manage

Once you have engaged your distributors and implemented a plan for the year, it is crucial for you to monitor its progress by managing your distributors. More often than not, companies forget to manage the program which, of course, means their success is frequently sabotaged.

Set the scene

It is okay to use a very down-to-earth approach to manage your distributors. Formalise the plan in a document – even a simple Excel, Word or Google document will do the job; you can use whatever format you want. Once you and the distributor have agreed on the yearly plan, you can simply share the plan with them formally by welcoming them to the program, attaching the actual program, and then setting quarterly performance review parameters from the outset. If you are dealing with the European market, you will need to start working with the distributor from October as a minimum in order for the program to kick off in January.

It's important to note that in Europe everything starts in January. In some sectors it could be as early as September; you will need to determine what timeframe you need to follow to be aligned with your industry.

Schedule performance reviews

In an ideal world, your distributor would roll out your plan perfectly and everyone would be happy. In reality, you will find that everyone – including you – is caught up in their day-to-day tasks and the program may become side-tracked or forgotten. Make a point of planning a strict schedule that includes a monthly informal update regarding how things are going. By following this process you will be able to detect any problems with rolling out the plan. Then, on a quarterly basis, the progress of every element of the plan can be reviewed.

You're in control

The beauty of this strategy is that you are in control! You can't control everything in the field, but you now have a simple way of tracking how you are going against your own sales targets. As a result, you can easily measure if the distributor is performing well or not. You now have the information at hand to evaluate if the distributor program is working, or if you need to change or adapt it. Have your targets been unrealistic? Has this lead-generation campaign produced the expected results? These are just a couple of the questions you can ask yourself to gauge progress.

Managing distribution

At this point, you have the relevant information to decide whether you need to increase your support to a distributor or, alternatively, whether you will need to add a new distributor in the market. In the worst-case scenario, you have the evidence to terminate your relationship with a distributor if things go wrong. For example, you are now aware if your quarterly evaluation of the distributor's key performance indicators shows they are not putting the necessary effort in. Of course, the first step is to try to find out why; you may then decide to not invest as much time with a distributor – or perhaps you need to invest *more* time with them – or to completely stop dealing with them.

* * *

From the information outlined above you should now have a much clearer picture of what a distributors' program is all about. The program will give you the tools to assess your sales channels and to indicate to you if you need to change anything in your approach to better support your distributor. It also gives you key information to determine if you need to add or let go of a distributor.

5 | MARKETING

Remember, it's all about sales!

When we take companies to Europe, we usually recommend our clients budget some marketing dollars to help us accelerate sales. Every investment they make in Europe must help us generate sales. Because we deal with small businesses, we like to focus on marketing activities and tools that help us get in the market, generate leads, show credentials and raise our clients' profile to secure sales.

Developing your promotional collateral

As we first introduce a product or a technology to the European market, we need to quickly trigger the interest of the people we are targeting. To get the conversation started, we need to share with them information that can quickly give them an understanding of the product. They need to grasp who this company is, what they provide, and the benefits of their solution. In addition, we need to reassure European prospects that the company is sound and has credentials.

To convince a European prospect to have a first conversation with you, you have to build the following collateral.

Company profile

If you are a well-established company in your home market, and maybe you are already active in other international markets, you should have a short company profile available to send to a prospect. It will help you build credibility.

You need to give information about your company such as date of creation, number of employees, capabilities, certifications and main customer segments. Don't go overboard – keep it very short. These days we are bombarded with too many e-mails.

If you are only a start-up or in early stages, be careful what you include in your profile. It may create some uncertainty in the eyes of your potential buyer. Having worked with Australian tech companies over the years, I have been used to playing up their strengths to convince European buyers. When they were young companies and their number of employees would seem too low in the eyes of their potential buyers, I would omit it. I would simply focus on their strengths, the benefits provided by their product, and their key clients.

Product brochure

Your product brochure needs to be professionally designed. Your marketing collateral will give the first impression to your European audience. Therefore, it needs to make you look like a multinational. It does not cost much to have a professional design done these days.

It needs to be short in terms of wording. Wordy brochures are just not read. And this brochure will be translated into multiple languages at some stage. The more words, the more expensive your translations will be. So, use icons and product photos to make your brochure visual.

The other advantage of going for a short brochure is that the PDF will be light, and this will increase your chances of getting your e-mail to your destination and actually read.

What your product is

In your product brochure, you need to outline in simple terms what the product is. Our clients are often selling very technical products. Typically, they will tend to explain what the product does in terms that are too technical, using jargon. All of us tend to be too close to our subject of expertise and tend to forget that our industry jargon does not make sense for people outside our professional network or people who are not exposed to our technology. You also have to put yourself in the shoes of a non-native English speaker.

You need to explain what your product is. If somebody was searching for your product on the internet, what terms would they use to describe it?

Key features

When describing key features, use the same general rule: short, simple terms.

Benefits for the users

With your target market in mind, outline the benefits for them. Ideally, if you can quantify a benefit that is best. Some of you would be familiar with pitching techniques, like your elevator pitch. In that type of exercise, usually to give impact to your pitch you need to substantiate your benefits with a specific, quantifiable outcome.

Don't make your list of benefits too long; you will lose the attention of the reader. If you have only three major benefits, for example, it will increase your chances of readers remembering them. Use words that are specific; avoid generalities.

Case studies

As mentioned in chapter 2, case studies are great to help convince potential prospects. Again, they need to be sharp and short. The fewer words the better. They can just be one page. Photos and videos are great for case studies, because they make your case study more real and more interesting. Have your logo on it and have some quotes. At least if your reader has little time to read your case study, she can see a logo, a quote and a photo of the product in use. For software, it may be just having a screenshot of your user interface with your logo. Anything visual of your solution in use is great.

Having your material translated

A very common question I get is: 'Should we translate our brochures into European languages, and if so, which languages?' Let's have a look …

At the Market Validation phase

Right at the start of your journey in Europe, when you are unsure of which country you are going to sell to, you do not need to translate your marketing collateral into all the European languages. English will be sufficient to start. At Exportia, once we have assessed that a company is ready to export to Europe, we conduct a market validation project, during which we establish which two European countries our client should focus on. For this, we don't require them to translate any of their marketing collateral, because we don't know yet where we are going to sell. We just need all the required collateral in English.

At the Lead-Generation phase

Once we know which countries we are going to focus on, then we require the collateral to be translated. It gets the message across more quickly. It also helps to build credibility in the eyes of the prospective customer or partner. And it shows a commitment to the market.

Recently I have done some presentations speaking in German or French over an English slide presentation. I have also recommended to an Australian professional speaker having her slides translated into French while she was doing her presentation in English. These 'in between' solutions are okay during the early days of establishing your business in Europe.

When we do lead generation, we often participate in trade shows. If this is an international trade show, we will check the nationalities of the international visitors and exhibitors. We will focus on the ones we are targeting and will translate into their language.

If we exhibit at a European show that has a national focus then we will just have our focus on this European country. We would usually also plan for a few English shows, as there are always a few European visitors.

At the Scale phase

When you start selling in Europe you are in the Scale phase, and you should have your collateral translated into the European languages you are selling to. Your distributors' sales team will need your collateral to sell your product to their customers. They will not use an English brochure – they would be embarrassed to do so. The same applies if you have a local sales team or agents.

Make it easy for your salespeople to sell. Give them the materials in their language.

The importance of owning your translations

I recently had a meeting with a new customer of ours. So far, they have sold successfully in Italy. To minimise their costs they had their Italian distributor do their translations for them. I think this is a clever way to get marketing collateral translated with the right specialist vocabulary from that specific country. However, they were losing control over the content being translated. Also, it means that control over the branding style may be lost, so the impact of the brand diminishes. They may have different designs and branding styles being distributed around Europe.

My recommendation is to get the translations done yourself and then get your European team to check them. They can give you feedback on the technical terms used. It might be more costly, but you retain control over your name, content and brand. You are sparing your business some potential issues down the track.

I also like my clients to keep the freedom to change distributors if they don't perform. Having control over your own marketing collateral makes it easy to switch.

Trade shows: the ultimate for European lead generation

At Exportia, at the same time every year we have our trade show season. We love these shows. They enable us to turbocharge our clients with leads and nurture our relationships with our distributors, partners and customers. This is clearly the most powerful marketing tool of all.

We usually consider a good return on one show for one of our customers to be gaining more than a hundred qualified leads by the end of the show. Less than that and we question if it's worth exhibiting on our own or whether we should just exhibit on our distributors' stands.

Interestingly, over the years we have found that the two most valuable types of shows are:

- European shows that are truly international

- specialised conferences.

Both work very well and bring very highly qualified leads for our clients. We then leverage these leads with our distributors. It shows them the product or solution can create new business for them.

The different types of shows

Major European trade shows

Major European trade shows happen between the end of August and early December. They are truly international; they drive visitors Europe-wide and even visitors from other parts of the globe. Some shows only happen every two years. You will note that a lot of the international shows happen in Germany. Germany is the powerhouse of trade shows – they host the largest European events.

Over the years, we have been very active at trade shows. For example, at the time of writing this chapter – December 2018 – we already know we will be participating in a minimum of five European trade shows, five conferences, and two national shows in 2019.

At the international shows, European distributors are often going shopping. They are looking for innovations or new products that will be the next thing, so it's good to use these shows when you want to set up your European distribution network.

In the cloud, software and digital sectors, I find it's more productive to exhibit at shows for the industry you are targeting. You will be more likely to meet your target customers. And you can detect the potential partners you may work with in future. The best way for me to check if we are selecting the right show is to ask our prospects or customers which shows they are visiting to look for our category of products.

And make sure you submit an application for an award if a show offers this opportunity. It's a great way to get exposure.

National shows

National shows are equally important; they enable you to gain good exposure to your local target market. They are great when you really want to kick off sales in a specific market. Because they are of smaller size they usually are more manageable and give you access to key partners quickly. Your key partners would usually exhibit at these shows.

Once you have a distributor in place, you may find it more cost effective to be present on your distributor's stand instead of exhibiting yourself. However, you won't have ownership over the leads when you work from a distributor's stand. It makes it harder to track the progress of the leads.

Conferences

There are several types of conferences that are really great to market your business. They are often cost effective. In some instances, they cost very little for exhibitors and your fee will also pay the cost of attending the conference.

Different types of organisations hold conferences. Industry associations often hold one, particularly in the medical sector, where often each specialty has an association of practitioners that holds an annual conference.

Influencers in your market may also hold a conference. For example, in the safety sector, in some countries the safety institutes or the work insurance companies are holding annual conferences.

Another interesting aspect of these conferences is the chance to submit a paper and to present. That is an excellent opportunity to build instant credibility and attract customers. It can raise your profile significantly.

I have also found over the last few years that conferences are a great way to build relationships with key influencers in your market. Conferences often have dinners and other networking events, which offer more opportunities to have conversations and get to know people.

Trade show logistics and planning

Having a successful show is all about good planning. Here is an example schedule of what to do and when. European shows may have long waiting lists, particularly the larger ones. Don't be discouraged by this long timeframe. Sometimes we register for shows at the last minute. Perhaps we only found out about that show at the last minute and we made the most of it. We were there with a low-key stand: a couple of banners, a product display and brochures, nothing fancy, and it was a success. So, we know we should attend next time, and we'll get in earlier.

12 months ahead	6 months ahead	3 months ahead	At the show	Within the 3 months after the show
Lodge your application	Inform your clients and prospects you will exhibit and offer for them to book a meeting with you	Booth location:	Scan everyone	Within a week:
Choose what type of booth design:		• be in your product category for people to find you	Ask them for their consent to be uploaded in your CRM	• send thank you for your visit e-mail
• you do it yourself	Book:	• be near the big players you want to align with	Ask them for their consent to register for your newsletter	Within 2 weeks:
• the show organisers do it for you	• book business card scanner	• be near the players that have the same product positioning as yours	Write down what documents you need to send them	• send all the documents and information requested
• low key: you produce banners, and hire booth furniture from the organisers	• book your passes: how many free visitor passes will you want to send?	Firm up your meeting schedule and locations: on your stand, on their stand or at a coffee place?	Write down what the next steps are	• schedule a follow-up meeting
			Rate every contact priority 1, 2, or 3	
			Greet your peers, introduce yourself to the team of local industry players that don't compete with you	
			If you are a CEO, ask for the CEO. If you are a salesperson, introduce yourself to other salespeople.	

12 months ahead	6 months ahead	3 months ahead	At the show	Within the 3 months after the show
Get information about awards: can you lodge an application for an award? Will there be any conference you can present at? Do you need to submit an abstract? Plan for a minimum of two people at these shows.	Will there be any press conference? Any presentation to the press?	Start a targeted digital market campaign on LinkedIn and/or Facebook to all your contacts, profile of your target market and people you like or who follow the show Translate the brochures in the languages of your target visitors and exhibitors Organise the shipment for your marketing collateral from a local European printing company (one month ahead)	Are there any award presentations? Which date? Check if there is any early bird price for booking next year's show Check out booth locations and where you want to be next year Write down things you want to do better next time	

The power of videos

Videos are very powerful for spreading your message, and are easy to create. There are so many ways you can use this media. I really like videos because they can easily be transcribed and translated. You can then display in the video the translated subtitles in the languages you need.

When you work in Europe you will have to deal in many different languages. Videos make it easy for you to explain a product visually, which makes it easier for a non-native English speaker to understand what your product is about.

Trade shows can be a great opportunity to shoot videos. With some of our clients we have shot some very short, simple videos on our stand in different languages, such as:

- welcome to our stand

- an interview with end-users about a product

- an interview with distributors

- a product demo

- a corporate video, such as a CEO interview.

Social media and Google Ads: powerful tools at your fingertips

Videos are powerful for attracting the attention of your European audience on social media. You can create more traction on your social media pages using videos.

Social media capabilities in terms of profiling are incredible. Social media agencies have the capability to target your European audience with Facebook or LinkedIn campaigns. We have experienced this type of campaign with specialised media agencies. They are truly powerful.

Here are some examples of online ads and campaigns you can work on:

- offer a demonstration of your product

- offer a free trial

- offer the opportunity for people to meet with you.

Too often companies build up a following on LinkedIn, Facebook or other social media but then don't know what to do with it. The reality is that followers are *not* leads and they still need to be qualified. These people you are connected with on social media may still need to be educated about what you do and still need to be engaged. For that you need to offer them some useful content. You can also invite them to meet you at an event or a trade show you exhibit at or a conference you present at.

Because of the language diversity in Europe, it makes sense to hire a local agency that can curate content for you in the language of the market you are targeting.

Leveraging influencers

Once you have identified which country or countries you will be focusing on, it is very valuable to have an influencer strategy. Influencer strategies have proven to be very efficient once you have started to sell. They can really take you to the next level.

You first need to determine who the influencers are in your market. Who does your target market look up to when it comes to buying your type of product?

Once you start to scale your sales in a given European market, you can use influencers to further expand your presence. This will only work once you have established a user base. These influencers will want to see some user base before they can confidently recommend your product. They will not usually recommend a product that does not have a track record.

I have come across different types of influencers. Let's have a look ...

Key customers

Having your product recognised by key customers or potential customers who are active in industry groups is an efficient way for a newcomer to get recognition in the market.

Key players in a given sector often form associations and steering committees. They join forces to exchange information about industry issues and best practices. These are often formed for the industry to solve a specific problem, such as new regulations on safety or major environmental challenges. Steering committees are often formed as part of an industry association. They can also be a chapter of an industry association.

Key opinion leaders

Key opinion leaders may not necessarily be your customers but are experts in their area and have a strong following. They tend to write papers about their work and present their findings to their peers at conferences. They often are keen to learn about and try new products. You can identify them easily as they have a high profile and are involved in their industry events and associations. Sometimes they even have management roles in these associations.

They are well regarded in their industry, and any product or solution they have tested and they recommend builds instant credibility. If they believe your product or solution has some value for their industry, there is a good chance they will recommend your product and share about it; for example, online, in articles or at a conference.

Regulators

Over the years we have also come across organisations that play the role of regulators for their industry. They are sometimes a government organisation, like a research institute for example. Others are a combination of industry representatives and a government organisation. They are influential for the industry as they establish regulations and best practices.

Government organisations often have to stay neutral and cannot recommend a specific product. However, what I have found really interesting is that they are often open to hearing about new products or solutions, and this is really helpful when you launch a new product from a new brand in the European market.

These organisations can really help you to build credibility in the market. They need to be seen as fair. When they conduct product evaluations, they want to make sure they include all the options available in the market.

Complementary products

Sometimes you will find allies that will help you get in the market. When you start Europe, you will lack brand recognition and you won't be a home-grown brand. In some markets, such as Germany, if there is a locally made alternative you will have to be significantly better and smarter to beat your local competition. Partnering with local allies is a good way to gain credibility, get better access to decision makers, and be recognised as being part of the local industry.

Here are a few examples …

In manufacturing

One of our clients is an accessory manufacturer for the automotive industry. Their market is very competitive, with many European players. It took us a while to secure some sales, however we were not happy that we did not grow sales much.

Our client had started to build a few relationships with car manufacturers in their home market. With our client we worked out that we should get the European automobile manufacturers to recommend their accessory. We were confident about the excellent quality of the product. So, we started to lobby car manufacturers to partner with them. We used the fact that a new European anti-pollution rule was about to come into effect which would be a significant issue, and this was relevant for our client's product.

To date, we have secured three official recommendations for our client's product from three major European car brands. This has raised the credibility of our client significantly. Car manufacturers have very thorough evaluation processes – they don't recommend a product unless it has passed many tests.

It was very powerful to be able to work with these multinationals and to leverage their network. It has driven significant growth. The car manufacturers were happy to recommend a product that they recognised to be of excellent quality.

In the machinery sector, we often find our clients are using parts in their machines that are manufactured by well-established and renowned manufacturers. It is useful for us to reach out to these manufacturers and have interesting conversations with them about potential opportunities for our customers in Europe. We have found all kinds of partnerships over the years in manufacturing that provided excellent leverage for our clients, from cleaning products to medical devices to machinery parts. The possibilities are almost endless.

In the software industry

In the software industry it's very easy to leverage partnerships. It is common practice. There are plenty of partner programs. Some of them are pure distribution or reseller programs (as in the sales channels chapter).

For example, a client of ours has developed a solution for the digitisation of forms. They are partnering with very large electronic signature providers. It has proven a very efficient way for them to get initial leads in the European market, as they had a previous relationship with these providers in their home market. We will use this channel to further expand their sales and their footprint throughout Europe.

It's very common for there to be complementary tools or software already well established in Europe. For example, if you are an SAP partner in your home country, you could draw on that relationship to enter a European market.

I have also found that the major global consulting firms, such as E&Y or Deloitte, could be good influencers for software companies. They tend to recommend software they trust and that fits with a particular tender they are bidding for. But, I have not pushed this type of partnership so much in the past, as they tend to have a lot of inertia. I always look for agile partners and not for partners that are going to slow my clients down. However, if you have already built a strong relationship with them you may not want to overlook this option.

Advertising in European magazines

Advertising in magazines tends to represent a smaller share of the marketing spend nowadays. The return on investment is hard to measure. However, if you target the magazine well, this may be an additional way to convey your message to your target market.

We usually pick magazines that can demonstrate that their audience matches the people we are targeting. We also systematically push some content to the journalists. Ideally you want to have an ad along with an article.

In some industries, magazines do product reviews. Others have awards as well. It can be a useful way to raise awareness about your product, and is a great way to qualify your audience.

Interestingly, most print magazines also have a good digital offering. They have built a nice following on their Facebook pages and are able to offer online campaigns. They also send newsletters to their readers, for which they usually have packages as well.

Use the opportunity of a trade show or a conference to identify the magazines and publications that are present. It's also a good chance to identify the journalists writing about your product area.

6 | TEAM

The people who will take you to success

One key element to being successful in the European market for a small to medium-sized business is your team. Very often, our clients compete with large multinationals. From the perspective of the European customer, what makes the difference between dealing with a large supplier and with a smaller one is usually the customer experience. This means that the team involvement, the quality of the service they provide, and their responsiveness can help make a relationship – or break it.

As small businesses, we don't have at our disposal massive budgets. However, we can easily provide excellent customer service, take into account a customer's desires, or fix a problem. We can also very quickly respond to a new customer request. The way you can really differentiate your business from very large, well-established competitors is with your awesome team.

We all know that larger businesses do not always provide great customer service. Requests get lost in the labyrinth of departments. Some of my clients are shipping directly from Australia to Europe, and we often get compliments from the European distributors on the quality of the service provided. It amazes me that sometimes they even tell us they get better delivery times from us in comparison with a large competitor that has a massive European logistics platform.

Everybody on deck at the HQ

To succeed in Europe, you will need to engage your entire team in the process. It's vital to underline the importance of the European market for the business, and the opportunity it offers. A business that exports successfully to Europe has more chance to become a major player in its industry. It makes a business more sustainable. It makes a business more attractive for investors.

A common mistake that small business owners make is they grow international sales by themselves and they don't involve their team. Consequently, their team cannot help, and it becomes very difficult to convert leads into sales. Leads grow cold, and European requests get forgotten. The business owner comes back from her trip and is inundated with requests from her team. And slowly the European leads get lower on the priority list, until they are completely forgotten.

So, everybody in your team must be on deck!

Staff involvement and motivation

At Exportia, we come across all kinds of different businesses. Some of them have exposure to international markets from day one. Others are prominent players in their home market and are looking at the European market for expansion – this type of business needs to be careful. It is a cultural change.

There are many ways you can involve your team in the expansion process. First of all, they need to be informed of the strategy. What is the plan for the business in the European market, and what potential does that represent? Then they need to understand what it means for them individually. What new tasks or new requests will they need to process? How will that impact their day-to-day role?

My first professional job was as a sales rep for a French small business. I was their Export Manager, and my first task was to open a distribution network in Germany. I drove 10,000 kilometres a month to create that network, and was one day a week at the office. One day the accountant comes to me a bit angry and says that there are plenty of new small orders coming in, and that the customer service team was complaining it was taking them too much time to process them. I was puzzled: wasn't this exactly what I had been hired to do? Create orders? Even though everybody knew my role, they did not quite comprehend what it meant in their day-to-day positions. Initially it will require some adjustment, and this change should be embraced by the entire team.

Your development in Europe also enables you to provide more opportunities to your team. They can travel and meet European customers. The business will grow, and so will your team. Some of your team members may be highly motivating by this and jump at the opportunity of international roles.

Customer support

Customer support is one of the first roles to be impacted. European customers who enquire or ask for further information should be looked after with utmost care. They should be responded to in a timely manner. It's important to always ask where customers found you. Any enquiry coming from Europe should be redirected to your sales representative in charge of Europe. Your sales representative should then contact them promptly to qualify the lead and look after it.

As a small business, you can't afford to let these enquiries go cold. Your sales team may have run a campaign, been to a trade show, or undertaken some other sort of lead generation. Now is the time to harvest these leads and convert them into sales.

It's so important to look after your first European customers and treat them like royalty. Good customer support will enable you to keep them as long-term customers and to grow the business with them. If you think in terms of cost of acquisition, these initial customers may have cost a lot of time and effort for your business. Don't let this go to waste because of bad customer service.

Technical support

Equally, technical support is critical for your success in Europe. In the early stages of your business expansion, you may not have a local European technical team. So, you will have to establish a system for your technical team to make sure European technical enquiries are not overlooked. They need to be treated with the highest level of priority.

You need to make the technical support smooth, so your European customers don't suffer from the distance. There are plenty of ways to minimise the impact of distance for your customers. Here are some good examples:

- **FAQs:** Of course this is the first port of call. If you can build a frequently asked questions database for your European customers, that is a great way to provide support. The only downside is the translation required to many different languages – it might be hard to maintain.

- **Online technical enquiry form:** This is a good option because you can track response times, and make sure somebody is actually taking responsibility for each enquiry. These days there are plenty of cheap ways to create online forms on your website.

- **Get your distributor to do your first-line support:** It's often possible to have this arrangement with your distributors. They can look after the enquiries from their customers related to your product, and have the option to pass on to you the more technical requests. The downside of your distributor or channel partner doing your first-line support is you don't receive the market feedback. A technical enquiry from the European market can mean different things: is this a technical problem you need to solve? Or does it mean there is a specific need for that market which you don't know about? Technical enquiries can tell you a lot.

Feeding back field information to research and development

The European market may have very different requirements to your home market. Inevitably, Europeans will ask for some specific features or for new products. It's important to tune in and listen to their requests and see if your product could benefit from some changes. It may create some opportunities for your business.

At the other end of the scope, you need to sell what you have now and cannot distract your sales team with products that are not ready to sell. Also, there will always be people who ask for new things, but in reality would not buy what they ask for or it only responds to a small need of theirs. So, there is an evaluation process to be followed to enable the R&D team to focus on the right business opportunities and not be distracted with new products that don't have a market.

One of the main advantages of smart and agile R&D teams is they can come up with solutions to a problem in a product. One of my customer's R&D teams excels at that. I remember being in Germany and having an issue with a product during a demo. I reported the issue immediately, and explained the problem to the R&D engineer in charge of that part of the product. By the time I was back in Australia, he had already found a way to improve the part and fix the issue. I was really impressed.

R&D teams can tune into the European market by visiting major European trade shows. It will enable them to understand where your competitors are at. Just a warning though: some researchers need to be briefed before roaming around a trade show. They need to be made aware of what can and cannot be said when they visit competitors' stands. You may feel the need to do that depending on the profile of your researcher.

Are sales agents common in Europe?

As you are growing your business in the European markets, there is an amazing way to expand your presence: hiring sales agents.

Having hired and managed sales agents across Europe, I am happy to share my experience. In the US, sales agents are very common. They are very often organised as agencies with large teams of reps. They may be called manufacturer's reps. It's quite a common business model in the US to manage and grow sales with distributors. In Europe, it is not as well established or sophisticated as in the US. However, in Europe sales agents do exist in a large number of industries.

They are a powerful way to grow your sales. Imagine having 10 or 100 sales representatives representing your product on a daily basis in their region, driving around and carrying your business card! On top of that, you would just have to pay them on a commission basis.

Be clear on what a sales agent is

A sales agent is a sales representative; however, he is running his own business. That means that agents are *not* your employees. They conduct their activities in the best interests of *their* business. That means you can't ask them to report to you like you would an employee. However, in practice, if you are working with good professionals, you will see that they will be keen to share as much information as possible with you.

Sales agents work for several companies – they can't be dedicated exclusively to one business. They will carry your business card together with those of other businesses. If you ask them to work exclusively for you, they can ask to be reclassified as an employee and ask for the associated benefits. The local tax office can force you to reclassify them as employees. You may have to hire them, as well as pay all taxes and social security contributions they are entitled to.

Familiarise yourself with local regulations around sales agents

Depending on the country, there may be established regulations, rules and practices around engaging and working with sales agents. When I established a network of sales agents in France for example, I often referred to the legal status of sales agents for help. It was great to have specific rules to rely on. For example, there is a simple standardised contract used to engage an agent. And if you need to terminate a contract with a sales agent, there are processes to do so.

An agent has the ability to sell his portfolio to another agent, and he must inform you if this occurs. If you want to cancel his contract, you need to buy his portfolio at a pre-set price. The calculations are made very clear in the regulations. It's very helpful to know from the start what you would have to pay if you wanted to stop working with an agent.

Rules such as this exist in most European countries, and are a great tool for you to refer to. If you need assistance, engage the services of a local lawyer.

What do they do?

Traditional sales agents usually support your distribution network. They are there to work with your distributors and push them to sell more of your product. They are making sure the distributor remains focused on your product at all times.

Sometimes agents provide quotes to their distributors on your behalf, following your approval of course. In other cases, you may just want them to stick to product demonstrations and sales activities. They can also visit end-users and generate leads for their distributors. The agents who are able to do that are the best ones in my opinion. They usually cover a specific region, and they are usually on the road four days per week, and sometimes five days.

How do they get paid?

As mentioned before, sales agents are paid on a commission-on-sales model. However, there can be other arrangements; you just need to check what's feasible within the local regulations. Most of the time they receive a commission from 5% to 10%, depending on the value of the product they sell. You don't pay for their travel expenses.

If the sales agents don't actually sell, you need to ask your distributors to provide you with the sales numbers per territory. This way you can make sure you pay your sales agents accordingly.

Where do you find agents?

That is a question I'm often asked. The truth is it depends on the industry. And they are hard to find, because they often are individuals. They are not easily visible as they carry other businesses' business cards. There are industries where sales agents are very common and there are industries where sales agents just don't exist. In Europe, for example, I rarely come across independent sales agents in the IT industry. They are more easily found for manufacturing.

There are many ways to find out if there are good sales agents in your industry in a given country. One way I often use is to contact my colleagues who are selling non-competing products in the industry, and I simply ask them: 'Do you use sales agents? And what is their level of professionalism?' Another option is to ask the distributors you work with. They will tell you if they are aware of any good agents.

Interestingly, for some of my clients I have found that the sales agents who came to us in the initial months of us introducing the brand to a market were not the right ones. We were only able to detect and select the right sales agents once we had established distribution and started to have good traction in the market.

How do you select sales agents?

The selection process is critical to your success with an agent. First of all, in my experience it does not work when you try to force a sales agent to do what they do not currently do in their day-to-day job; for example, asking a sales agent to focus on visiting end-users when they usually spend their week visiting distributors. If you take them too far outside their comfort zone and their routine it usually won't work.

The best way to check how they work is to contact the companies they currently have a contract with. Ask the sales agents for details of people they are currently 'repping' for. You then ask those people how it is to work with that person on a daily basis.

Your distributors will tell you if they get good support from them as well. Also ask them if they know other sales agents. The more candidates you have, the better.

How do you manage sales agents?

Good sales agents are usually excellent professionals who are autonomous in their work. They usually do not require a lot of management. Of course, they need support, and their requests must be responded to promptly.

They will add a lot of value if you invite them for a yearly planning session. They are in the field all the time and so have valuable feedback. They will tell you what you need to do to grow your sales.

If they don't work out well for you, you need to plan regular catch-ups and reassess if their business model fits with your goals. Ask them if they feel they are still aligned. Try to take this opportunity to learn. Why is it not working with that agent?

I once had to stop a sales agent selling one of our products. I had a good working relationship with him, but he simply could not sell our technical product; he was much more comfortable selling simpler and higher volume products. He did well with another brand and wanted to focus on that. He also did not have the patience for the long sell cycle required. Basically, he wanted to get in, do the sale, and get out. It was clearly not the best fit.

Because we had a good relationship, he did open up about that, and he introduced me to potential successors. At the regional level, he was the best person to know who's who in the small sales agent world. I did really like one of the candidates. I interviewed the agent, and the due diligence checks came back with very positive feedback.

The two sales agents worked out between themselves the sell price of the portfolio, and it went very smoothly. The new agent worked out to be a much better fit.

When you decide to end a sales agent contract, there are usually steps to follow. The easiest process is for your rep to sell her portfolio to a successor. Of course, you need to interview and make sure you like the new rep. Otherwise the option is also there for you to buy back the portfolio from the agent.

Hiring in Europe: the costs and the risks

In my business Exportia, we often get companies referred to us. Our partners or our clients talk to a company that is active in Europe. They see they have been unsuccessful so far in Europe or are frustrated they are not generating enough business.

Quite frequently, when I have a discussion with these companies I find they have hired a local team member and it did not work out. It's a very frequent mistake small businesses make in Europe: they hire too soon.

When a large business launches into a new country, it's fine for them to recruit locally straight away; they create a local subsidiary, and they hire the services of local accounting firms, often from the local branch of their current very large accounting firm. They have the budget to secure every step, and to survive any costly mistakes along the way. They can afford trial and error; they have all the advisers they need and the big money to pay them.

Most importantly, because of their brand and the salary packages they offer, they are able to attract the right talent from day one.

But when a small or even a medium-sized business comes into a new market, they face several hiring challenges. Let's have a look at these …

Challenge 1: Europe has some of the lowest voluntary staff turnover in the world

Small businesses have to build credibility in the market to be able to attract the right people. And people who are talented all currently have jobs. To make them change and work for you, the offer has to be very compelling. In Europe, staff tend to change jobs less frequently than in the rest of the world.[1] According to Mercer, a global HR consulting firm, in the tech industry the global average of voluntary turnover is 9%. European countries tend to be below this average.

---

1 2016, Study from Mercer: https://www.mercer.com/content/dam/mercer/attachments/global/webcasts/gl-2016-webcast-talent-tackling-trends-in-turnover-mercer.pdf.

In comparison, Australia is above the global average, with 9.5% voluntary staff turnover, as per the National Salary Survey[1] conducted by the Institute of Managers and Leaders in 2017. In the US and Canada, the North America Mercer Turnover Survey[2] found that this figure was 14% in both countries. Some of the highest voluntary turnover rates are in South America – with Argentina at 16.8% and Venezuela at 16.7% – and in Asia – with the Philippines at 15.5% and Indonesia at 15.7%.

The only European exception is Romania with 16.5%.

Therefore, to be attractive to a European staff member, you need to have a good case. You will need to show that your business is in the European market for the long term and that the opportunity is attractive. The decision to work for your business needs to be seen as low risk.

Challenge 2: The risks associated with hiring in Europe

We have already worked out that you need to have an attractive offer to recruit talented people, which tends to be difficult when you are just starting in the European market and you don't have a track record. Among the customers that come to us, very often they have recruited in the initial stages of their launch in the European market, but at this stage small businesses usually don't have enough financial backing to bear the risk of failing.

When launching in Europe, small businesses hire too soon

Here are some insights from companies that hired their own staff locally in Europe and did not obtain a good return on their investment. These companies have shared with me openly why this option failed for them.

---

1   The National Salary Survey 2017, https://managersandleaders.com.au/National-Salary-Survey/.
2   The North America Mercer Turnover Survey: https://www.imercer.com/content/article/employee-turnover.aspx.

Company One had a large investor funding their launch in the European market. It allocated a large investment to promotional activity and the hiring of a UK-based senior executive in their industry. The business team members knew that person from a professional connection.

After two years of intensive promotional activities in Europe in numerous countries, the business found that the French and Scandinavian markets were picking up. Several distributors started to show interest. The UK-based team member had no experience in these markets. He would travel back and forth from the UK to France with an interpreter to talk to distributors. His feedback to HQ was that the European distributors would not take stock and would refuse to pay for freight inside Europe, and they refused to pay import taxes. That was why he could not get them to start buying. The business was at risk of shutting down, having made a large investment with no return.

The board implemented several drastic measures to turn the situation around. They appointed a new CEO. They dismissed the UK-based sales representative, which was a long and costly process. We came on board and were mandated to look after the French market. The CEO and Global Head of Sales looked directly after Scandinavia. The first thing I audited were the trading terms. I knew that European and French distributors had no problem at all buying from outside Europe. They do that on a daily basis. So, I renegotiated the trading terms, trained the distributors, and they started to buy. It took me six months to get the business going. Within two years, they reached a million euros in turnover, and that is when they organised the first recruit in France. Company One then had a better understanding of the dynamics in the French market and was in a much better position to manage that person, which I did on their behalf before I recruited a sales director for France and moved on to another country.

Company Two had hired a German manager to run their German operations and established a subsidiary. It allowed them to secure **OEM** contracts with German manufacturers. When they were ready to expand the business, they started to feel that the German manager was not at ease about getting out, doing lead generation and making cold calls. This is what the company needed at the time.

When the time came for the hard discussion with the manager for him to move on, it cost the company 250,000 euros, given his seniority.

Lessons learnt from these stories:

- don't hire too soon

- know your market before you recruit somebody in that market

- don't assume that somebody based in the **UK** will have the ability to develop the entire European market

- use channel partners and distributors to generate your first million euros in sales, then hire to take your revenue to the next level.

Summary of the risks associated with hiring too soon: 'Gambling with time and money'.

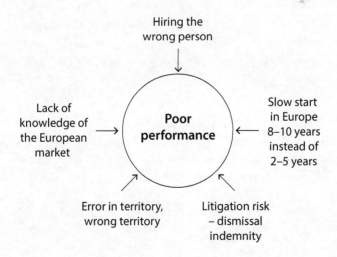

Risk 1: Gambling with time

The main risk for a small business is taking too long to generate revenue, and not being able to get a return on investment soon enough. This is what happens when companies hire the wrong person. Hiring the wrong person means you won't get the result you want, or you will get it at a much slower pace than you should.

It may mean you have to hire someone else, so it takes time to go through the recruitment process again, probably three to six months. After that, this person needs to be trained; it will take three to six months again to get that person fully operational. It means it may take you an extra six months to a year to have a salesperson fully operational to generate revenue.

Sometimes you hire the right person but your team has not built sufficient knowledge about the European market yet. It makes it harder for the management team to manage a salesperson. Same thing for the salesperson; they are going to take some time to generate interest. So, while they are an additional cost for your business, they have pressure to work out how to start making the first sales without having any credentials in the market. It can be hard for them and it will take them more time to get the business running.

We have worked with businesses whose turnover was around one million dollars. For this size of business, and even beyond that level of turnover, it's critical to get quick success. Otherwise, it may jeopardise the life of the business. Over the last 13 years, I have seen businesses with a lot of potential at risk of not achieving the results they expected.

Hiring a European sales representative without having a lot of experience or prior knowledge about the market also makes the small business very reliant on that person. Your small business relies on that person's skills, expertise and knowledge of the European market.

Another typical mistake is in the allocation of territories for your salesperson. I think this error can significantly slow down your business growth in Europe. As per the example of Company One, and as per my experience with Australian companies entering Europe, Anglo-Saxon companies tend to hire British citizens to look at the European market. The typical mistake is to hire a British citizen, based in the UK, only to work out down the track that the German market is the best country for your business. Now you have a non-German speaker who has little experience in Germany in charge of making the revenue take off in Germany. That person will probably focus on the UK market, which is not the right one. It will take you a few years to work this out. The better alternative to become successful would have been to have done your homework and found out first that Germany was your market, and then to recruit a German person.

If your European sales representative ultimately does not help you generate the sales you need, and you are unable to train that person into it, then it is time to look at options to dismiss your salesperson. To minimise the risk and ensure fairness for your European employee, you need to seek legal advice. A local lawyer will clarify with you what the process is and things you need to be aware of. They will make sure you have done everything the right way.

As a benchmark, hiring the Exportia outsourced European Sales and Marketing team often enables our customers to avoid these mistakes and to pave the way before we help them build their team in Europe. As we are active in most European countries, we are able to assess where to start, generate the first leads and close the first sale in a timely manner. We follow our 4-Step methodology that will be presented to you in more detail in chapter 8.

In terms of timing, this is how we unfold our methodology. In the first year the Export Readiness Diagnostic is conducted, as well as a Market Validation and a Lead-Generation phase. Then a Scale phase starts. The Export Readiness Diagnostic (step 1) is free and can happen within 20 minutes. We look at your capabilities to make sure you are able to succeed in Europe. If your business is ready to go further, then we undertake a Market Validation phase (step 2), where we help you select the top two countries for your business and assess which country to focus on, and establish if you have potential by gathering feedback from key players in the market, such as potential sales channels and potential end-users. This usually takes three to six months.

In the Lead-Generation phase (step 3), which lasts six months, we generate the first leads for your business, we secure and train your sales channels, and we usually either obtain trials or your first sale in the market.

After that, we want to Scale (step 4) your business to your first million euros in sales and beyond. This is where we will start to look at building your team to scale your presence in Europe.

Exportia 4-Step methodology

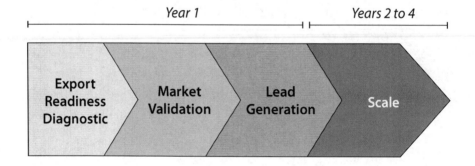

Risk 2: Gambling with money

Let's look at the numbers. I thought it would be interesting to compare the cost of hiring in Europe for a small non-European business with working with a company like mine. Our philosophy at Exportia is always to be a safe alternative to hiring in Europe and to provide results more quickly. Recruiting in Europe is quite an engagement when you have to set up a subsidiary. The employment contracts are not as flexible as in Australia or in the US, for example. This has been confirmed to me many times by my customers. However, for a new exporter it's important to look at the facts and figures.

In the tables later in this chapter you will see two examples. I have picked two major markets from the European Union; for the first case France and for the second Germany. I have chosen them because these are the two largest markets we at Exportia are active in. Therefore, we have ready access to very reliable information.

In both cases, I have picked a four-year period to compare as it's a realistic time within which hiring a first employee in Europe is usually considered.

Usually, if your business does recruit in Europe, I would recommend recruiting a sales representative as opposed to a more senior person, the reason being you need that person to be in the field and be a go-getter. They need to knock on doors and be on the road, planes and trains. Sometimes, a sales director would not want to do that; they will want to hire a team. It can sometimes be difficult to fund a full team to start with. Hence, my recommendation to recruit a sales representative to get the sales started. You can manage them by providing support from the head office and by travelling regularly to Europe.

I have indicated the cost of hiring a sales representative both in France and Germany. We have taken the hypothesis that the sales representative has a minimum of five years' sales experience in the country.

Costs of hiring your own European sales representative

The cost of hiring your first European sales representative comprises:

- **The cost of a setting up a subsidiary:**[1] To hire an employee in Europe, it is most likely you will have to establish a company in Europe. The local government will charge an incorporation fee. You will also require a lawyer to register the company and publish the company status. You may also require a shareholder agreement.

- **The cost of managing a Europe-based subsidiary:**[2] You may want to budget for annual legal fees if you need further legal advice – to publish details of your annual general meeting, for example.

- **The accounting costs:**[3] I have added into the study the accounting costs of running a subsidiary. Of course, they will depend on the type of accounting firm you pick. The Big Four will typically be more expensive than a smaller or a mid-tier accounting firm. I have chosen to pick a small to mid-tier accounting firm's costs.

- **The cost of recruiting an employee:**[4] Recruitment fees will mainly depend on the type of recruiter you choose. If you choose a well-established recruiter like Michael Page, for example, then their fees will of course be higher than a smaller, boutique-type recruiter (for example, Talescence in France).

---

1   Me Edith Bon, BIA Avocats, Montpellier, France; Dr Stephan M Ebner, von Seelstrang & Partner, Muenchen, Germany.
2   Me Edith Bon, BIA Avocats, Montpellier, France; Dr Stephan M Ebner, von Seelstrang & Partner, Muenchen, Germany.
3   Marie-Anne Pillot, Solis, Nantes, France; Gerd Fuhrmann, Falk Co, Heidelberg, Germany.
4   Cora Heckelmann, Michael Page, Frankfurt; Myriam Deschamps, Talescence, Paris.

We see value in both approaches:

– A competent boutique-style recruiter may do an excellent job, with very reasonable fees.

– A well-established agency such as Michael Page may give you the exposure you need to attract a larger number of candidates.

   Then you may have two ways of being charged by a recruitment company:

– Success fee only: You pay 10% of the annual gross wage of a sales representative once the candidate has been hired. This type of service provider has a large database of candidates.

– Head-hunter type of fee: Typically from 15% to 35% of the annual wage. You get charged one-third of the fees at signature, one-third at the presentation of candidates, and one-third when securing a candidate. The head hunter looks for the ideal candidate for you, even targeting candidates who are not specifically looking but who are perfect for the job.

   I have also added the marketing costs of recruiting, such as posting ads on social media platforms such as LinkedIn.

- **Drafting an employment agreement:** You will need a lawyer to help you draft an employment agreement that complies with the local workplace laws. Each European country has its own way of classifying each job category. Under each category, the employee is entitled to specific benefits. There is also a definition of typical working hours, what overtime is, and what the rules are around leave. It's important for you to get guidance on these details early on.

- **Salary:**[1] I have chosen a profile of a sales representative who has experience of more than five years. For your first recruitment you need someone with experience who can be quite autonomous. You do not need a very senior person at this stage, as you need someone who will be able to build the sales from scratch. They will have to open doors and be on the road. The salary reflects this profile (around 50,000 to 55,000 euros gross). As a comparison, recruiting a sales director will start from 90,000 euros per year.

- **Government tax on wages:**[2] In Europe taxes vary greatly from country to country. In France, you have to pay 41% of the gross salary, while in Germany it is only 20%.

- **Car leasing:**[3] This is a requirement for a sales representative. It is expected to be included in the package. Be aware that in Germany owning a nice-looking car is extremely important. It's more important than in France. In a very competitive job market like Germany it may make the difference. Therefore, I have allocated a higher budget for a car rental for the German scenario. I have chosen a compact car for France and a higher standard for Germany.

- **Payroll costs:**[4] There are costs associated with managing tax on wages, keeping track of paid and unpaid leave, and so on. I have added this cost as well in the study.

---

1   Michael Page: Salary Survey, Sales and Marketing 2019 Survey for Germany; L'étude de remunerations 2019 for France.

2   Marie-Anne Pillot, Solis, Nantes, France; Gerd Fuhrmann, Falk Co, Heidelberg, Germany.

3   France: Arval online simulation tool for a 24 months period and 72,000 km per year; Germany: real life example from an Exportia client.

4   Marie-Anne Pillot, Solis, Nantes, France; Gerd Fuhrmann, Falk Co, Heidelberg, Germany.

Costs for hiring a sales representative in France

	Year 1	Year 2	Year 3	Year 4
Salary 1 sales representative	50,000	51,000	52,020	53,060
Taxes on salary (% on gross salary: 41%)	20,500	20,910	21,328	21,755
Marketing cost of recruitment	3,950	–	–	–
Recruitment costs	17,500	–	–	–
Drafting contract	1,220	–	–	–
Car leasing	7,860	7,860	7,860	7,860
Cost of a subsidiary	–	–	–	–
Incorporation	2,500	–	–	–
Lawyer fees to register company, create status	3,000	–	–	–
Annual legal assistance	–	3,000	3,000	3,000
Accounting costs	2,000	2,000	2,000	2,000
Payroll accounting (1 employee)	500	500	500	500
Total	**109,030**	**85,270**	**86,708**	**88,175**

Costs for hiring a sales representative in Germany

	Year 1	Year 2	Year 3	Year 4
Salary 1 sales representative	55,000	56,100	57,222	58,366
Taxes on salary (% on gross salary: 20%)	11,000	11,220	11,444	11,673
Marketing cost of recruitment	3,950	–	–	–
Recruitment costs	19,250	–	–	–
Drafting contract	1,500	–	–	–
Car leasing	15,000	15,000	15,000	15,000
Cost of a subsidiary	–	–	–	–
Incorporation	1,200	–	–	–
Lawyer fees to register company, create status	4,000	–	–	–
Annual legal fees	–	3,000	3,000	3,000
Accounting costs	3,950	3,950	3,950	3,950
Payroll accounting (1 employee)	960	960	960	960
Total	**115,810**	**90,230**	**91,576**	**92,950**

To be realistic, I have also added as an indication the cost associated with a dismissal.[1] I thought it would be important to include this information. Recruiting is a difficult task and sometimes the person you hire does not meet your expectations:

- **Getting some legal help:** If you are unhappy with the performance of your employee, I strongly suggest you get some local legal help to make sure you follow the right dismissal process. When I discussed this with a number of lawyers, basically their response was their legal fees would depend on the case. Of course, it's very hard to give a response. In France Edith Bon and in Germany Dr Stephan Ebner expressed the same view. I have chosen to give you an optimistic view and to take the hypothesis that you will only require two hours of legal support to come to an agreement with your employee.

- **Severance payment:** This amount will vary by country. As I write this book, the general rule to calculate it in France is: one quarter of a yearly salary per year of service for the first 10 years of employment, and one-third from the 11th year onward. In Germany, it is equivalent to 50% of the monthly salary per year of service.

- **New recruitment:** Of course, if you dismiss someone, you are going to have to recruit a new person. That is why I have added further recruitment costs.

---

1   Dr Stephan M Ebner, von Seelstrang & Partner; Edith Bon, BIA Avocats.

Risk of dismissal in France

Euros: between 34,450 and 71,950	After 1st year	After 2nd year	After 3rd year	After 4th year
Indemnity 1/4 of gross salary per year of employment. After first year.	12,500	–	–	–
Indemnity 1/4 of gross salary per year of employment. After second year.	–	25,000	–	–
Indemnity 1/4 of gross salary per year of employment. After third year.	–	–	37,500	–
Indemnity 1/4 of gross salary per year of employment. After fourth year.	–	–	–	50,000
Legal fees (best case)	500	500	500	500
New recruitment	21,450	21,450	21,450	21,450
Total	**34,450**	**46,950**	**59,450**	**71,950**

Risk of dismissal in Germany

Euros: between 37,450 and 78,700	After 1st year	After 2nd year	After 3rd year	After 4th year
Indemnity 1/4 of gross salary per year of employment. After first year.	13,750	–	–	–
Indemnity 1/4 of gross salary per year of employment. After second year.	–	27,500	–	–
Indemnity 1/4 of gross salary per year of employment. After third year.	–	–	41,250	–
Indemnity 1/4 of gross salary per year of employment. After fourth year.	–	–	–	55,000
Legal fees (best case)	500	500	500	500
New recruitment	23,200	23,200	23,200	23,200
Total	**37,450**	**51,200**	**64,950**	**78,700**

Costs of engaging the services of Exportia

In the Exportia cost example, we include the implementation of our 4-step methodology. This methodology is explained in detail in chapter 8. The objective of the Exportia methodology is to take small and medium-sized businesses to their first million euros in sales and beyond.

For several reasons, it's hard to compare what we do at Exportia with a scenario where small businesses recruit by themselves. We usually work as a team on each project, we provide lead generation, customer service and pure sales and business development. And this is usually delivered by a team. Moreover, our team is multilingual and multi-nationality, therefore we can cover a number of countries at a time. It makes it hard to compare it with one employee recruited in one country. In addition, we usually proceed gradually as we proceed on a step-by-step basis.

Indicative fees for the 4-step methodology

Step	Exportia fees in euros
1. Export Readiness Diagnostic	Free online tool[1]
2. Market Validation	17,000
3. Lead Generation	25,000–35,000[2]
4. Scale	Retainer + Commission From 40,000 euros to 150,000 euros[3]

Here's what's included in the Exportia scenario:

- Year 1 includes: some desktop research, research phone calls, a lead-generation campaign, customer and partner visits, a sales representative and multilingual customer service.

---

1 http://diagnostic.exportia.com.au/7pillar/
2 Depending on the number of countries covered.
3 Depending on the size of the team Exportia provides and the territory covered. We usually require a three-year engagement.

- From year 2: for the Scale package: we provide a team composed of sales representatives, multilingual customer service team, lead generators, and a sales director.

Things to note about comparison Exportia fees with the cost of hiring one Sales Representative in either France or Germany:

- I have excluded bonuses and sales commissions. They depend on company policies, so are hard to give a general rule about. I have done the same for the Exportia scenario. In order to keep things equal for both scenarios, I have not included the commission that is usually included in an Exportia Scale package (step 4).

- In the sales representative scenario, we have included a car package which is not present in the Exportia scenario. In the case of Exportia, we usually share travel expenses among several customers of ours, which reduces our travel expenses for our customers quite significantly.

- The Exportia package is scalable as it allows you to add more countries and more salespeople in the field in multiple countries quite easily.

- In the scenario where you recruit your own team, if all goes well, you have to plan for a second recruit towards year 3 or 4.

Building your European sales team successfully

The advantages of hiring once you have built up sales

The knowledge advantage

Let's look at the advantages of building your knowledge of a market before you hire. As I mentioned earlier, having done business successfully in the European country where you are about to hire is a great way to increase your chances of making your recruitment a success.

You can better guide your sales representative if you know what needs to be done to take sales to the next level. You will be known as a representative of your company. This is a safety net for your business. If anything is not right with your new recruit, the player in the market that you have developed business with and that enjoyed working with you will contact you and tell you.

Not everyone is able to start a new position afresh with no direction. Having somewhat grown your market, you will be able to organise a handover of contacts, and assign priorities for your new recruit, so it's a much better way for them to start. They can begin with these assigned tasks to get some traction. Then, if they are quite senior, they can quickly ramp up and take it to the next level. If they are the right candidate, they can then define their own priorities and plan next steps easily and rapidly.

You can also check what information comes back from the market. Having sufficient understanding, context, and contacts in the market, your representative knows you have the ability to reach out and see how things are going.

When I hired a sales representative in France for one of my clients, we already had a good presence there. We had achieved a million euros in sales and already had a network of distributors and sales agents throughout France for this client. I knew the distributors well, they were convinced about the product, and were happy about the growth this new product generated for them. To take it to the next level, I needed more field presence, with a sales representative who would regularly visit end-users to grow the sales and support the sales agents as well as distributors.

This sales representative came from one of our distributors; he was highly motivated because he had already sold the product. This sales representative is still with my client and is doing really well. When I on-boarded him, I knew the distributors and the key accounts. Whenever there were issues with the sales representative, I received feedback about it. And I was able to train him into his role, providing feedback and working with him.

The established player advantage

I've had many interesting experiences with recruiting European sales teams, for Exportia and for my Australian clients. My best recruitments were always when I had sufficient knowledge of the market and when I was in a position to make an attractive offer. Making an attractive offer to a salesperson does not always mean offering a generous salary package, although you have to be in line with the market you play in.

You also attract better talent if your business has started to achieve some sales. As I mentioned earlier, good salespeople already have a job! They will only switch if they have an offer that's very attractive to them.

Interestingly, one of my best recruitments was for a European Sales Director. I had developed the sales for one of my clients for a particular country; for about two years, I was carrying the business card of Sales Director for this client's business. I was mingling with my peers regularly at trade shows. We would also call each other from time to time to talk about agents, distributors, and key accounts. Of course, these people worked for non-competing businesses, but I chose them because the positioning of their product was aligned with my client. My goal was to recruit a Sales Director to replace me and take the sales to the next level. For that, I needed somebody who could sell a technical product and who knew what premium positioning meant. I needed a hunter as well, not a farmer.

My client was ready to recruit, and so I started to signal the market that we were going to recruit someone senior to grow the market. I signalled the market by informing my distributors, sales agents, and my peer network. And all of these people were able to give me a few names. And then, I also had targeted several peers that I did get along well with and I thought would have the right attitude and the right contacts. I thought they would fit in with my client's company well, and also they would be flexible enough to work for a small business! Every time I interviewed a salesperson who had worked for a large multinational for a long time, or almost all of their career, they really did not fit. Even if they claimed they were flexible, the reality is they were used to some level of comfort! Too much comfort is not likely to happen when growing a small business in a new territory.

Interestingly, among the peers I was targeting, several showed interest in applying, and one of them sent me one of his previous collaborators who was changing jobs. This way, I started to build a small network of potential candidates. I did meet all of them about the job, but I was in no hurry. I could continue to grow the market as I came closer to recruiting. Ultimately, I choose to propose only one candidate to my client, one of my peers whom I had observed for almost two years at trade shows and had him occasionally on the phone to talk business.

He turned out to become an excellent sales director. I chose him because he already knew the network I had built and he had contacts and relationships beyond that. He was ambitious to grow to the next level, and was frustrated not to have the right opportunity with his current employer. He was trusted by the market, I had received good feedback, when I conducted due diligence. Anyways, I had observed him for two years and knew what people thought about him already.

The funny thing that I realised after having recruited him, was that from his position he was an observer of our activity in his market. When we then became colleagues and started to exchange about what triggered his interest: he had been observing me and the way the company was growing for the last two years. He was looking for an opportunity to go to the next level in his career, he wanted more responsibility. He liked the way we presented the company in the market. He saw that the company was growing very fast, year after year he saw the progress, he saw an opportunity for him to grow too. He saw the fast growth agile side of the company, which I translate to being a small business, and he saw that it could give him some opportunities to really contribute. He liked our conversations, we were aligned, we got on well. He also like when he talked to the other people in my client's management team. The package was in the market rate and so he was sold.

A more solid revenue base to bear the cost of a dismissal if needed

If anything goes wrong with a recruitment and you need to pay legal costs, indemnities and so on, you are better off already having some revenue coming from that market. Ultimately, if a recruitment does not work out, you will need to hire again. You are in a better position to do so if you are established in the market.

The attributes of a good sales recruit

I've taken dozens of companies to the European market, and all of them were non-European small and medium companies. They were companies that had a strong R&D component to them, such as being in software or biotechnologies. They all had a premium product. Their sell cycle tended to be longer, and more technical, with a trial phase. In most cases, they had little or no sales in Europe before they came to us.

Having worked with many companies with that profile, I developed a profile of the best sales candidates for my clients. Let's take a look …

Hunters

Hunters have no fear of picking up the phone, driving throughout their territory, or opening new doors. It's in their DNA. Salespeople who have spent too much time in the office doing reporting all day are not usually suitable for entering a new market.

Flexible for small business

They have to understand what it is to work for a small business. They won't have a large marketing department looking after their every need. Sometimes they will even have to come up with their own marketing. They also need to understand that small businesses cannot usually offer large packages like multinationals can. They need to be excited to work with a small, agile and dynamic team.

That involves some level of risk and uncertainty, but they have to find this aspect exciting. I always prefer candidates who know small business.

Tech lovers

Depending on your product, the salespeople you hire may need to fit this bill. A technology product, whether it is a piece of machinery, a clever device or software, improves the life of a worker, saves lives, saves money, reduces carbon emissions, and so on. And reading this book, you are likely to fit in that category.

Being tech-lovers, they will understand the cleverness of the product, and why it's positioned as premium. They understand premium, and can sell premium.

Long sales cycle

When you sell a technical product to a new market, there is a sales process to follow. First, the demos, then the trials, and then the sales conversion, and after that the aftersales checks and service, and the customer care. It will be slightly different for each company, but it will usually be a longer sales cycle that requires persistence.

Your sales representative needs to understand and like this type of sales process to be a high-performing sales representative for you.

Has a good reputation, is trusted and has contacts

Of course, what really is a strong indicator of success for you is if that person is liked and trusted in the industry you are playing in. It brings results more quickly, they don't need time to build rapport, and they are already an insider. They already have the contacts, so they can just get on with the job.

* * *

Sometimes it won't be easy to find candidates with this profile if you start afresh in a market. But again, if you build your sales first, as per my recommendation, you can do it.

The Exportia Model

In the cost study earlier in this chapter I highlighted the financial benefits of using the services of Exportia in comparison to hiring your own sales representative.

Exportia provides an outsourced European sales and marketing department for non-European technology businesses. We only work with small and medium-sized businesses. We have Europe-based sales teams that set up Europe-wide distribution, sales agents and key customers. Once our client is ready, we start hiring on their behalf. This reduces their risk in the early stages of their development in Europe. And because we know European markets so well, we are able to transfer that knowledge to our clients very quickly. As a consequence, they can build up their knowledge about the European market and their network of contacts much more efficiently. It de-risks their business. We can rapidly scale up or down in case of unexpected circumstances.

We have the capability to work in any European country. That gives businesses a wide reach. We also train their new team members as if they were our own salespeople. We on-board them as well.

Generating one million euros per year revenue enables them be in a financial position to hire, and at the same time it gives them the financial means to bear the risk. They can afford to pay for legal costs or indirect costs due if a person turns out to be a low-performing team member.

Recruiting without a subsidiary

Over the years, I have come across companies that provide outsourced payroll management. They provide the opportunity for companies that do not have a subsidiary in Europe to hire European staff members. This solution enables a non-European company to be compliant with their obligations towards their employees for their social security contributions and with the required taxes on wages.

It can be a good temporary solution depending on the country where you hire.

This solution has some limits. European tax offices don't like companies to generate revenue in their market for too long without getting their fair share of tax. If the revenue starts to be significant, the local tax office will certainly try to check if a company based in Europe is paying company tax in Europe, or if all the profit is transferred to a non-European country.

Most small businesses start small in Europe and need to seek fiscal advice as they grow. Things change constantly in this area and need to be watched and considered on a case-by-case basis.

7 | DASHBOARDS

For high-performance European sales teams

At Exportia we love our dashboards. We love to report on our progress to our customers in dashboards. We find that they keep us focused on our sales goals, accountable and honest. We can quickly identify what works and what does not. It allows us to detect delays and bottlenecks and act upon them.

There are many advantages to working with dashboards.

Our customers need to have a clear vision not only of how they track on their sales but also on their finances. Small businesses that want to grow in the European market need to have a clear vision on the investment needed to support their export effort in Europe. Succeeding in the European market won't work with a shotgun approach. What works is a steady long-term approach. You need the required level of investment and that needs to be a five-year plan, or at least a three-year plan.

There are plenty of advantages in articulating clearly an export plan with clear targets and the budget needed to enable you to reach your goals. It's a great way to focus your team on the right objectives. Sales teams are best managed with clear objectives and key performance indicators that support your target.

Articulating a budget to support the realisation of your vision will enable you to identify gaps. You will also be in a better position to prepare your application to get government grants or investor funding if required. Small businesses often have a short-term view of their finances, but you can only drive to success companies that are committed to the European market in the long run and that have allocated a suitable budget for it.

The revenue side

Simple sales indicators for your sales team

Monitoring the progress of your sales team during your initial stages in the European market may be tricky. You need to adapt the key performance indicators (KPIs) depending on the stage you are at. You may have a limited pipeline of opportunities, or you may just be at the stage when you need your team to build a pipeline of leads.

Focusing on the right clients

When you start in the European market, you may want to track the ability and the progress of your sales team in generating new leads.

You also want to make sure the leads your team generates match your ideal customer profile. You are much better off having fewer leads of better quality than a large quantity of leads that are not the right clients for you. If you do that, your sales team will spread themselves too thin and will waste time before they get their first sales. To describe the type of clients you want your team to focus on, you can use the ideal customer template.

Monitoring early wins

What I have often done for my clients, when we just started for them in Europe, is focus on getting initial trials in the given European country we were focusing on. Monitoring the number of trials, tests, proof of concepts, or whatever you call it is a great indicator of how you are going.

It also has the advantage of breaking things down into smaller steps. It makes targets more achievable for your sales team to focus first on trials, rather than having a huge sales target to achieve. Ultimately, the trials with the right profile of customers should lead to sales.

Number of new distributors

Along with an overall sales target, track the number of new distributors you are appointing. At times, increasing sales just means having more distributors on board. If this is the right time to give a push, having KPIs around the number of new distributors secured is a great way to grow your sales. It helps your team focus on the right indicators to achieve their target.

I've had clients that found it risky to be reliant on a limited number of distributors. We then gave ourselves a target to appoint three more distributors during that year.

Useful examples of key performance indicators for sales representatives are:

- number of product demonstrations
- number of leads with ideal customers
- sales targets
- number of new distributors.

Once you have defined your KPIs it's important to formalise them and to have a formal kick off. Your sales team needs to be on board. They need to think about them every day and remember to focus on them. Then KPIs need to be looked at with each team member at least quarterly.

Sales results and forecasts

Often small businesses lack the tools to provide reports back to their team. What sales teams are often complaining about when they work for small businesses is the lack of visibility on their sales.

151

They like to see how they are tracking, and if that deal they were working on signed or not. And it's hard for a sales manager to provide you with a sales forecast if you don't give them visibility on their results.

What's important is that your sales team provides you with clarity on how they track. That requires a level of trust between the sales team and their manager. When they report a sales lead to you, they may not know if it will convert. You need to get a feel for the likelihood of a lead becoming a sale. That is obtained through transparent communication and trust.

It's a great idea to enable the sales team to report on their deals while giving them the ability to flag the chances of winning. As your team works on these deals, they can move the deals into a more certain category, such as 'active' or 'likely'. Most CRMs give you the ability to qualify your sales opportunities with a percentage likelihood of winning the deal at different stages. And a sign date is always great to report on.

Sales forecasts – quarter 1

Company	Product	Euros	Sign date	Chances >75%
Pharma GmbH	X Ray Blue	1,000,000	30/11	90%
Medicinale SpA	X Ray Orange	300,000	15/10	75%

Company	Product	Euros	Sign date	Chances 50%–70%
Pharma Red SAS	X Ray Yellow	750,000	30/11	50%

Company	Product	Euros	Sign date	Chances ≤50%
BigPharma Ltd	X Ray Blue	1,000,000	10/12	50%
Medicinale SpA	X Ray Yellow	750,000	15/10	20%

To get the actual information from your sales team, they have to trust that you will not hold them accountable on deals that are impossible for them to sign. You are always better off knowing what the real deal is, rather than pressuring your sales team into impossible targets. Ultimately your sales team will tell you what should be done to make their target.

Sales performance management for distributors

Where most small businesses fail with distributors is when they don't hold them accountable and they don't monitor their sales. They just wait and see! And not surprisingly, the performance is poor.

Your distributor's sales teams are like an extended sales team. In the early stages, you need to guide them on what your expectations are. As much as possible, apply the same method as per your sales teams: make sure they target the right profile of clients. It will help them secure deals. A good method is to focus them on that profile at the time of training; you can then motivate them on each trial or lead they generate with that ideal client profile. As they grow sales, you want to give them some key performance indicators on the number of new leads they generate.

Some of your distributors will dislike your request to have key performance indicators established. Some distributors will even resist communicating about their end customers. But to make them successful you have to work with them at the end-customer level. This is the best way for you to generate sales.

When you start working with them, you need to establish KPIs to protect your business as well. If they don't perform it gives you a way out. It also gives the right focus to your distributor. You have to push them to work together with you on defining their KPIs and on monitoring them. The trick is really to make the system quite simple. Don't make things too cumbersome for them or for yourself.

When you establish a new distributor, that is when you need to establish the KPIs. Or if you feel it's too early at the start of the contract, you include the fact that KPIs will be defined after the first six months.

At the time of appointing distributors, the KPIs can also be around number of sales representatives trained, for example. It can also be around marketing events, such as a trade show or conference, a customer breakfast or a newsletter. You can find ways to push them to actively market your product at the start of the relationship. Once the distributor is more active, you can add leads and sales-related KPIs.

Sales performance management for sales agents

Sales agents run their own business and therefore don't have an obligation to report to you. However, sales agents who are good professionals usually are good at reporting.

They usually have excellent market intelligence, and they are valuable contributors to your team. You can manage their performance with key performance indicators, whether it's around clients you would like them to target or distributors you would like them to work with.

What usually happens with good sales agents is they will tell you what their indicators for the year should be. They know their territory very well. When I set up a network of five regional sales agents for one of my clients, I used to get them together once a year. This is when we would define the key performance indicators for the following year. I would then plan a six-month phone or web call to regroup on the indicators with everyone. During the year, I would talk to them monthly to check how they were tracking against their plan.

The same applies for a sales agent and for a salesperson – this is about setting goals, and tracking how it goes, and supporting along the way, and at the end of the year reviewing what the goal was, what was achieved and why.

Running high-performance sales meetings

During my career in sales, I have often participated in sales meetings and accounts planning. At IBM, as a rep, these sales meetings would take place on a yearly basis. They would be aimed at bringing the entire sales team together to coordinate our focus on one key client and plan strategic directions. For the last 13 years, at Exportia I have mostly organised, contributed to or led sales meetings with sales agents in Europe and with sales teams across the globe.

Here are the most important lessons I've learned to make sure your sales meetings are productive, motivate your sales teams, and are actually implemented.

Tip 1: Handle any issue or discontentment before the sales meeting

Sometimes your sales team, whether they are sales agents or your own employees, may need things, they may have some discontentment or specific problems. That happened to me once with a network of sales agents I had appointed for an Australian client in France. They were needing a lot of new marketing collateral and a lot of support, and some discontentment had emerged. So I spent an hour with each of them individually, and I let them raise their concerns. I then summarised and brought the list of concerns and queries back to the CEO. We then addressed and responded to each and every one of them. Then I did a wrap up with each agent in a brief phone call.

Now we were ready to start planning a sales meeting in a positive manner. Had we not done that, the sales meeting would have drowned in complaints and we would have been unable to plan for the year ahead.

Tip 2: Allow some time for the team get to know each other

Have a get-together the night before the first day or after the first day's work. You have to adjust to your audience; choose a venue or an event that will suit your team and allow them to get to know each other in a more relaxed environment.

Tip 3: Get all the participants to present

It's important for everyone in the sales team to present where they are at in a concise way, and what they are planning for the year ahead. Sales teams, whether they are all in the same building or across several countries or continents, crave information: they want to hear about success stories, and they want to hear what worked well in terms of sales campaigns.

Tip 4: Find leveraging activities

Find activities or a theme that all team members would be interested in and organise an activity around it. You could get them to sit down and brainstorm how they could target a specific industry, or which distributors they could target to launch a new product.

Tip 5: Keep the group accountable

This is the most important part. It's all about the implementation! Accountability is key. Make sure that when everyone leaves the meeting they are really clear on what their next steps are. It can be articulated in a three-month plan, then you can schedule a phone call with each participant to track the implementation of the plan on a monthly basis.

Tip 6: Learn from it

I recently conducted a sales meeting with a client and we made a point to debrief about it. We realised maybe not everyone should have been in the room. We'd had a very busy couple of months and we did not prepare enough in comparison to other sales meetings we'd held in the past. It's great to reflect on this and improve for the next time.

The expenses side

Creating an export budget (a five-year plan)

To create your export budget, you need to check several elements that are going to help you implement your strategy. The type of costs you will incur will vary depending on the stage you are at in your export journey. We will look at the costs that occur in the initial stages and then what you need to plan for down the track.

First, let's look at the initial costs when you are either starting in Europe and have no revenue, or until you generate several hundred thousand euros of revenue.

Typical costs when your European turnover is below one million euros

On page 165 you will find a sample budget for typical costs when your European turnover is below one million euros, and I will now explain these figures to you. I have gathered figures from our own experience as well as from our partners (accountants, lawyers, printing companies …) to give you a broad budget of what it takes to really grow your sales in Europe.

Team

Sales team

First look at your sales team; you may have dedicated resources for your European sales, or you may tap into your existing team to start with. If this is a dedicated resource, add their full salary to your budget. If it's a shared resource, determine the percentage of their time they spend on your export project and add this share of their salary to your budget.

In that budget line, you may have the export manager, the international sales manager, and a sales director.

Customer service

This is the same for customer service; you may have a dedicated resource or a shared resource. Allocate the salary of this person to your budget. If you don't have a customer service person for the European market, think about budgeting for one. This is an important resource to have on your side.

Engineers or technical team

The same mechanism applies for your technical support, or in some instances it may be your engineering team. Are they dedicated full time to your export project? Most of the time they are not. Allocate a line for technical support; this is critical to your success. For our clients who are manufacturing or developing technical products, having a technical person is a key to success in Europe. Initially, you probably won't have a resource based in Europe; it is often an in-house resource that will support European customers.

When you establish your European market, you need to support your European customers. Providing them with high-quality technical support will build trust. You want to provide them excellent support in order to make them forget they don't have a technical resource at their doorstep. You need to find an engineer or technician who will be happy to work odd hours with the time difference and is keen to travel.

Travel

Travel is an important one to plan for. Travel budgets are not always easy to estimate precisely; there are always things coming up, such as a client needing support or a new lead. It's important when you start to export to Europe to really be there for your new European customers.

For example, our clients at Exportia are Australian businesses. Initially, when I started Exportia and I had no team based in Europe, I would travel to Europe myself each month. European customers would see me as regularly as they would see local competitors. They really did not have the feeling that the company was based in Australia. And that's the perception you want to create. You want to ideally have several people travelling to Europe to look after your European customers.

Your first European customers are the most important; they are your leveraging tool. You need them on board for the long term. The way you do that is to visit them regularly.

Estimate your travel budget by starting to allocate the dates of your trade shows and conferences; usually you will already know your travel dates. And then add trips in between to make sure your European clients have regular contact with you. Conferences and shows are a good way to group several meetings at a time. You will need a minimum of two people per trade show. The only exception to that is small conferences.

Don't forget to plan the travel for your sales team as well as technicians and engineers. And sometimes someone else might need to jump on the plane too, such as the CEO. If you are the CEO and are doing the sales, make sure you involve other people in your team. Otherwise, European customers are going to think your business is too small.

Cost-effective European travel

The highest travel costs often occur during international trade shows. Very often, you would have that international show or conference happening in Germany. It will seem like the whole world is flying there and booking hotels. Plane tickets and hotel rooms become incredibly expensive during such times.

To get the best possible prices for accommodation during trade show seasons, make sure you book a minimum of six months in advance. In the last few years, we have opted for Airbnb with my team during trade shows; it is very affordable. During the rest of the year it may or may not be convenient, but it's a nice way to keep your costs down as a small business.

Generally speaking, booking flexible tickets such as for train and plane travel is the best option, even if they are more expensive at first. Meetings can run late or be rescheduled; you may get stuck in traffic. You want to have the opportunity to take the next plane or train if needed at no extra cost, or for a minimal fee.

Always check train options; it's the most cost-effective way to travel in my view. Nowadays highways in Germany are unpredictable with traffic, while trains get you where you should be on time, and you can work on the trip. You can be very productive on the train!

European high-speed trains travel at 300 km/h, so it's a great way to travel. I really like the Paris to Frankfurt line. You can travel from the centre of Paris to the centre of Frankfurt, getting rid of the commute time needed to go to an airport.

It's really hard for me to give you a rough travel budget as I don't know where your company is based. However, I can tell you that for us at Exportia, usually our travel budget is 45,000 euros per year. For each project, we usually have two people travelling. I'm based in Australia, and travel as often as once a month to Europe. We also have salespeople based in Europe who travel throughout

Europe all year around. We usually split the cost among several clients to make it cost effective.

You really have to do your own calculations. It's quite easy nowadays to plan your travel budget. You have plenty of websites that can help you with the costs of hotels, trains and flights, as well as rental cars.

In Australia, we work very well with our travel agent Flight Centre. Our travel consultant is now very familiar with our requirements. It's been very efficient to work with them as our itineraries are fairly intense and complex.[1]

Marketing

Brochures and banners

Brochures are still popular. You need to add the cost of brochures to your budget.

To keep costs down and to avoid the process of import clearance into the European Union, I suggest you find a printing company based in the EU that will manage all the printing and dispatch of brochures, banners and any other printing need you have.[2] You should be able to easily send the files for printing online.

Plan a budget for printing brochures every time you have a trade show or a conference. Nowadays, visitors prefer to have a brochure sent in an e-mail. However, you should still print at least 100 brochures for a three-day show. You need to plan for at least two languages: one brochure in English, for international visitors, and more importantly a brochure in the language of the location of the show.

In my experience, banners are also very useful to have at your disposal in Europe. You can print a few and provide them to your distributors for their marketing needs. Then usually what we do is we borrow them from time to time during the year. The European

---

1 In appendix B I have included the details of some travel companies that will be able to help you with your travel arrangements.

2 We have used an excellent service provider over the years. They are called Jextern, based in Lyon, France. They speak excellent English and provide services Europe-wide.

distributors are often okay to send them to you and then you ship them back once you have done your show.

Trade shows and conferences

Trade show costs vary greatly depending on the size of the show. Let's have a look …

International shows

European shows that have international exposure are the most costly. Sometimes you have to book them two years in advance, and there is a waiting list. The most cost-effective way to exhibit at international shows for small businesses is to book a smaller stand and have it professionally designed. Then you can have a larger impact for a smaller outlay. You should add more to the budget if you want to have a better design for your booth. The cost for a small 10 m^2 booth at a five-day show with a design provided by the organisers is around 10,000 euros.

Hotel prices reach crazy levels during the trade show season. Include accommodation for two of your team members, which is the minimum.

In terms of budgeting, the registration fees will need to be paid in advance, sometimes one year prior to the show date. The hotels will need to be booked six months in advance. So plan your budget accordingly.

Don't overlook Airbnb as an option to book accommodation when prices of hotels are looking crazy. However, nothing beats the convenience of being located walking distance from the show. You minimise all the delays, traffic issues and cost of a rental car. This is my favourite option.

Conferences

At the other end of the scale you have smaller conferences, and they are usually cheaper. It would cost you from 1,000 to 5,000 euros to exhibit. Then you can bring banners and have a table there. They also have nice sponsoring packages.

In your budget, you must have a mix of both types of shows to really help you generate leads and sales rapidly. Plan the dates well in advance, and plan your budget, otherwise you may miss out.

Advertising

Magazines

When your business generates less than a million euros in turnover, I would recommend not investing in advertising in magazines. The return on investment is too hard to measure. I would spend my marketing euros on other media.

Social media

In Europe, Facebook is widely used, and Facebook campaigns work very well. The key is to have the right targeting. For that, you need to know what your target audience looks like: what industry bodies do they belong to? What companies do they work for? What is their role?

LinkedIn is also widely used and is a good platform for advertising. France has a specific platform called Viadeo, but it's losing ground in favour of LinkedIn. Germany has Xing, which is still quite strong and widely used.

Generally speaking, you cannot go wrong with LinkedIn to target European professionals.

Allocating a budget for a social media campaign is a good idea. Start small and check the efficiency of it. Social media is amazing as you can track the success of your campaign. Customers of Exportia have allocated social media marketing budgets during trade shows to drive more traffic very successfully.

Translations

For translations, we have a schedule of fees from English to European languages, which is updated usually once a year. Translations are charged at a per-word rate. Translating a 2500-word brochure from English to German, France, Spanish or

Italian would cost about 575 euros per language.[1] Initially you may have two brochures to translate into two different languages. Let's take this as an assumption for your budget.

Lead generation

Lead generation is what is going to make your sales in Europe kick off. This is the good old *get on the phone, have sales conversations, generate the lead and close it!* Where small businesses often fail is during the Lead-Generation phase and when it's time to close deals.

In our experience with Australian small businesses, it's hard for them to build sales remotely, unless they plan a solid visiting schedule and work efficiently with sales channels to deliver the sales.

I have included a budget for market validation and lead generation. I will detail in chapter 8 what they are. Basically in our methodology, when we take a small business to Europe, we usually help them validate their top two priority markets and identify their channel partners in these top two countries.

In the Lead-Generation phase, we start to generate the first leads and engage with channels to get them to the first sales.

This Lead-Generation phase is critical on the path of your success in Europe.

Legal

You will encounter a number of legal fees, even at the start of your export journey.

Trademark registration

It's important to budget for the cost of registering trademarks in Europe. If you can afford it, I would recommend registering your trademark in all of the European Union. Even if you focus on one country at a time, you may have competitors that come from another European country and are active in the country you are targeting.

---

1 You can check out our translation rates by sending an e-mail to me at christelle.damiens@ exportia.com.au with the subject TRANSLATION and you will receive the link to our current translation rates.

Always keep control of your intellectual property and don't let any distributor or partner register your trademark for you. I have heard too many horror stories when companies have let their distributor register their trademarks in Europe. Then the distributor turns out to be inefficient and the relationship ends. What happens then? The distributor owns the company trademarks in Europe.

If you can't afford to register all of your European Union trademarks in one go, you have the option to register them country by country, as you go.

Distribution agreements

European distributors, particularly large ones, will probably ask you to sign their agreement. I would advise you to get a commercial lawyer to review these terms with you and budget for it. These contracts are often very tough on the supplier. The best way to work with your lawyer on it and minimise costs is to go through it in detail and mark up all the clauses that seem unfair or hard to fulfil. Basically, give a feel to your lawyer about what is acceptable in your eyes. It will minimise cost.

Sales agent agreement review

Sales agent contracts are usually fairly standard and short. They are quite straightforward. Still, the first time you come across one of these agreements you may want to have it checked by a lawyer.

Typical costs when European turnover is below one million euros

Team	Euros
Sales team (time spent in Europe 20%)	10,600
International sales manager (time spent in Europe 100%)	60,000
Customer service support (time spent in Europe 20%)	6,667
Engineers/technical team (time spent in Europe 10%)	6,000
Total	**83,267**

Travel	Euros
Travel budget	45,000

Marketing	Euros
Brochures and banners	
Printing	
100 x brochures x 4 pages	1,140
2 x banners (310)	620
Translation 0.23 x 2,500 words	2,300
Trade shows	
One international show in Oct/Nov/Dec	
Space 10 m^2	2,400
Booth design (furniture + light)	1,500
Parking	125
Hotel (5-day show; 2 pax)	4,000
One conference	
Registration fees	2,000
Shipping brochures and banners	200
Advertising	
Social media campaign	2,400
Lead generation	
Market validation	17,000
Lead generation	28,500
Total	**62,185**

Legal costs[1]	Euros
Search and registration EU-wide	350
Register TM (per country per TM)	500
Review of distribution agreements	2,000
Creating a distribution agreement	3,500
Review of sales agents agreements	500
Total	**6,850**

Total	**197,302**

---

1   Information kindly provided by lawyers based in France, Edith Bon, BIA Avocats, http://www.bia-avocats.eu/equipe-bia/ and in Germany Dr Stefan Ebner, von Seelstrang & Partner Partner http://www.vonseelstrang-partner.de/en/who-are-we/stephan-m-ebner/

Typical costs when your European turnover is greater than one million euros

When your business starts to generate one million euros of revenue and more, it will be time to think about structuring your presence in Europe. At some stage, you will need to have more people to support your sales. And to hire them you will need a company. You may not need to do everything at the same time.

I have indicated costs for Germany and France in the budget table. You are probably wondering why I'm only giving these two options. I had to make a choice, but still wanted to give you options. In my view, it's always best to have an entity in the country where you have the most activity, or very close to it. Therefore, Germany and France are good options. However, there are plenty of others.

I would also consider the Netherlands, for its convenient location near major markets and its close ties to the UK. The Netherlands is easy to deal with for English speakers. And they have plenty of schemes to encourage companies to have their European entity based in the Netherlands.

Having a UK-based entity means you will need to have an EU-based entity anyway. Having a local entity is important in a country such as Germany. However, it does not carry so much value in other countries. I would say having a German entity will facilitate your business in Germany. In the eyes of the rest of Europe, it does carry good brand value as well.

All the previous costs for less than one million euros in sales are still valid – we'll now look at the extras you'll need once you get to this point.

Having a local sales team

It's time to hire! When you start reaching one million euros in sales and above, it's time to hire your first salesperson in Europe.

In this first local recruitment, you may either decide to hire a senior person or a more junior person. The budget you will need to plan for the salary will vary depending on the country you are hiring in and the seniority of your salesperson.

I have indicated several salary scales for different levels in my cost study in chapter 6, Team. I have included these figures in the budget.

Ideally, you want to have the best possible pool of candidates. And therefore, you need to budget for some recruiters' fees. I've made recruitments with and without recruiters, both methods successful. However, I do enjoy the fact that recruiters have access to a large pool of candidates we would not have access to otherwise. Large, established recruitment firms usually have high-quality candidates reaching out to them. Even if you have a favourite candidate, following a recruitment process is still good practice. You are increasing your chances of finding the perfect candidate.

As I mentioned before, in Germany the job market is really tight, so you may need two rounds of recruitment before you get to the right person. In other European countries, it's much easier to recruit, because there are more candidates available.

Creating and running a European entity

Registering a company is usually quite straightforward. I have indicated the cost of doing so in Germany and France in the budget table.

I have also added the accounting costs of running it. It covers tax, payroll and general accounting.

European logistics platform

In most cases, having a European logistics platform is not necessary to grow your business in Europe. We have developed multi-million euros in sales without it. And this has been true with most of our clients that have a unique positioning and are not so sensitive to price. When your product has a real added value or provides a great return on investment, your customers are happy for you to ship to them air freight. They can sustain that cost.

However, when you play in a very competitive market, and you have to compete on price, then it may make sense to differentiate from your competitors by offering fast delivery. This also adds the complexity of managing stock in an additional location. It does also add cost. So, my recommendation is to look at logistics platforms when you really have no other option.

Budget scenarios

In these scenarios, which you may have recognised from chapter 6, you will also need to consider adding:

- additional travel costs
- the costs of your team at your HQ that will be supporting the local teams
- costs of hiring additional staff in Europe as you develop your sales, which you will certainly need to do
- costs of a logistics platform.

Typical costs when European turnover is above one million euros[1]

Germany: Cost of setting-up a subsidiary and hiring your first Sales Manager

	Year 1	Year 2	Year 3	Year 4
Salary 1 Sales Manager	55,000	56,100	57,222	58,366
Taxes on salary (% on gross salary: 20%)	11,000	11,220	11,444	11,673
Marketing cost of recruitment	3,950	–	–	–
Recruitment costs	19,250	–	–	–
Drafting contract	1,500	–	–	–
Car leasing	15,000	15,000	15,000	15,000
Cost of a subsidiary	–	–	–	–
Incorporation	1,200	–	–	–
Lawyer fees to register company, create status	4,000	–	–	–
Annual legal fees	–	3,000	3,000	3,000
Accounting costs	3,950	3,950	3,950	3,950
Payroll accounting (1 employee)	960	960	960	960
Total	**115,810**	**90,230**	**91,576**	**92,950**

France: Cost of setting-up a subsidiary and hiring your first Sales Manager

	Year 1	Year 2	Year 3	Year 4
Salary 1 Sales Manager	50,000	51,000	52,020	53,060
Taxes on salary (% on gross salary: 41%)	20,500	20,910	21,328	21,755
Marketing cost of recruitment	3,950	–	–	–
Recruitment costs	17,500	–	–	–
Drafting contract	1,220	–	–	–
Car leasing	7,860	7,860	7,860	7,860
Cost of a Subsidiary	–	–	–	–
Incorporation	2,500	–	–	–
Lawyer fees to register company, create status	3,000	–	–	–
Annual legal assistance	–	3,000	3,000	3,000
Accounting costs	2,000	2,000	2,000	2,000
Payroll accounting (1 employee)	500	500	500	500
Total	**109,030**	**85,270**	**86,708**	**88,175**

---

1   Figures provided by: Cora Heckelmann, Michael Page, Frankfurt; Dr Stephan M Ebner, von Seelstrang & Partner, Muenchen, Germany; Anval; Gerd Fuhrmann, Falk Co, Heidelberg, Germany; Myriam Deschamps, Talescence, Paris.

Do you need funding for your export project?

With the export budgets I have just prepared for you, you now have a clear picture of the costs involved in expanding into the European market.

The reality is, if you don't invest sufficiently you won't be able to generate revenue quickly. I have had cases of clients that have been quite timid in their investment in Europe in the initial stages. So, it took us longer to get them off the ground.

It does not mean you should be spending with no reason, but there is a minimum investment required to get results.

Government grants

Government grants can often be accessible through local, state or national government bodies. Our clients in Australia are typically accessing funds to support their export effort through Austrade. For non-Australian readers, Austrade is the Australian Trade and Investment Commission. It runs the Export Market Development Grants (EMDG) scheme, which is dedicated to supporting mostly Australian small and medium-sized enterprises in developing their exports. It reimburses 50% of a set of expenses. It has a set period within which to apply. There are several criteria to meet to be eligible. This eligibility criteria list is updated on a yearly basis; you can find it on the Austrade website. The link may change from time to time – if you search for EMDG eligibility criteria, you should easily find the most recent details.

Our clients can typically access other grants through other government bodies that are focusing on fostering innovation and promoting the commercialisation of intellectual property. These government bodies, such as AusIndustry, have development funds to promote innovation internationally. It's worth investigating. These organisations often fund market evaluation projects.

Local governments also have export programs. They often subsidise market research or travel expenses, for example. They are usually smaller funds.

Raising funds with investors

Venture capitalists love companies with international growth potential. It really showcases that your business is able to scale. When I have the chance to present to potential investors on behalf of clients, I focus on the size of the European opportunity, where we are currently at, where the wins are, and how we are planning to seize the European opportunity. This is a good option for you to consider. The European market is great to leverage with potential investors. I often like to say that companies that succeed in Europe have a chance to become a major player in their industry. And I mean it.

8 | THE 4 STEPS TO GET TO YOUR FIRST MILLION EUROS IN SALES

The Exportia Method

Getting ready to go to Europe

This chapter is where everything we have looked at so far comes together. I will go through how the Seven Export Pillars from chapters 1 to 7 are used in the Exportia methodology: the 4 steps to take your business to its first million euros in sales.

The objective of this methodology is to lower your risk and maximise your sales in Europe. I built it based on all the mistakes small businesses that come to us typically have made. It's based on our successes with our clients and what consistently works for them.

The 4-step Exportia Method takes all the guesswork out of your export process into Europe. It puts your business on the right track. It saves you time and money.

The 4 steps are:

1. First, you make sure your business is ready to go to Europe. You will have the resources and do the relevant checks before you start. This is the **Export Readiness Diagnostic**.

2. Then I will show you how to validate that there is a market for your product in Europe. No surprise here: it's called the **Market Validation**! This is where you select your top two European countries and get feedback from major potential distributors and end-users. At the end of this phase, you will know if your product has potential or not. If not, you will know why and will be able to act.

3. The next step is the **Lead-Generation phase**; once you have feedback from two European markets and positive feedback about your product or solution from distributors in these markets, then it's time to generate leads and get to your first sale.

4. Once you have started to generate your first sales, you now have to **Scale** your business to the first million euros. In the Scale step, you are industrialising your approach and turning initial sales into sustainable long-term sales for your business.

Step 1: Export Readiness Diagnostic

In the Export Readiness Diagnostic, four of the Seven Export Pillars are addressed:

- Dashboard
- Product
- Team
- Customers.

I have also added a few benchmarks based on what my customers are doing well, and on the things we do that work particularly well.[1]

Dashboard

We first look at the Dashboard Pillar.

Five-year sales target

Do you have a sales target for the European market for the next five years? It's important to have a long-term objective for the European market. Your level of commitment will determine your level of success. The European market requires a long-term commitment to be able to succeed. The European market is a major market; give it the attention it deserves.

You can determine your revenue target based on your competitors' presence. What realistic market share can you expect to achieve? I know it may sound a bit tricky to determine a sales target, but it's important for your business to realise the potential of the European market. And to place the right emphasis on it.

Export budget

Given the size of the European market, a realistic export budget must be allocated to make it happen. I have already given some indicative budget figures in chapter 7, Dashboards.

What's important is to confirm that you have the financial capacity to invest in Europe. If you are still a start up, your main focus should be to secure your first customers at home before you venture into Europe. No one in Europe is going to buy from you if you have no customers. It's cheaper to secure customers in your domestic market rather than in Europe. You need to generate sufficient revenue or have access to sufficient funding to enable you to work on the European market before you get any return.

---

1   The diagnostic could be a very short section of this book. I could just tell you: go online to http://diagnostic.exportia.com.au/7pillar/ and there it is! Within 20 minutes, you would have your report outlining your business's percentage of readiness, and with your personalised 'to-do list' you would know what you need to do next!

Funding options

When you prepare your export budget, you may realise that you need some funding to enable you to have sufficient resources to implement your plan. A lot of businesses manage to fund their international growth with the revenue generated in their domestic market. But that's not always the case; you may require some extra funding. You can check what government funding options are available. Often governments have programs to support small businesses to grow internationally. And raising capital is often on the cards for high-growth, high-potential companies.

Product

Compliance

Compliance is not optional. Your product must be compliant with European requirements if you want to sell in Europe. If you have a physical product, the most common European standard to comply with is the CE Mark. In fact, most products cannot be sold in Europe unless they hold a CE Mark.

This is a critical step before you start prospecting in the European market. The first question potential customers or partners are going to ask you is: do you comply with European norms and standards? If not, then they won't even want to talk to you.

Let me say it again: it's illegal to sell products in Europe that don't hold any European certification.

If you are not familiar with European regulations, get a certification organisation such as TÜV or SAI Global to evaluate your product and get the certification process underway. They will tell you which norms and standards to comply with.

An important piece of advice before you launch your product is to be conservative with the certification process timelines. Don't expect this will be a simple and straightforward process. It usually takes several months to have your certification process completed, and you may need to plan for up to a year.

Another important point is to have your certification body established in the European Union.

To be compliant with European Union requirements your user manuals must be multilingual. It does not mean you have to get your manual translated into the 24 European Union languages. However, you have to get it translated into the language of the country that you are going to sell in. If you are selling online to many different European countries, you will have to get these translations done in the languages of the countries you sell to.

Don't forget to make your user manuals as visual as possible. Engineers love very long and detailed manuals, and I can understand why. For very technical products it's important for your customers to know how to set up your product, and avoid mistakes. In some cases, you also need to write a number of statements that will protect your business against misuse of your product. You need to add warning messages. I understand all that, but at the same time remember you will need to translate it into a number of European languages.

Software and digital products don't follow the same process as those needing physical certification, but must meet other obligations. The General Data Protection Regulation (GDPR) that came into place in May 2018 may have an impact on your software application. We already have been through this in previous chapters.

In the case of software, you also may be required to store data in the European Union. This is a very typical requirement for European companies.

The same applies in terms of data security; check what the Europeans require in terms of protection of data and encryption, particularly for sensitive applications (such as banking, large-scale personal data collection, or health-related information).

IP protection

Generally well respected in Europe, your intellectual property (IP) still needs to be protected. You also need to make sure you don't infringe anyone's IP.

There are multiple ways to protect your intellectual property. Your intellectual property strategy can include a combination of trademark protection, patents and copyrights. Trade secrets are also common. Trademarks can be registered Europe-wide thanks to the Madrid Protocol.

Product positioning

Your product positioning needs to be ready before you start to prospect in the European market. Often companies I start to work with only have a limited view of their competitors. It's really important to know your European competitors. Your potential customers will ask you how you compare to them.

Direct competition as well as indirect competition must be looked at. Indirect competition sometimes is harder to beat than director competitors. Indirect competition is often a way of doing things that is not quite the way your product does, but it enables your customer to achieve an equivalent result. In the software industry, you would often compete with an internal software team that are employees of your client. They may be able to develop equivalent functionalities to your software package. In that case, you are competing with a department at your own customer; it's not an easy task.

The competitor search enables you to articulate your points of differentiation. Your differentiators will be very useful when starting your approach in Europe.

Of course, your pricing should reflect your positioning. Being more expensive than your competitors is absolutely fine, but it needs to be justified.

To help you articulate your differentiators, you can adapt the table below to your category of product features and benefits.

Product features and benefits

	Your company	Competitor 1	Competitor 2	Competitor 3
	Product name	Product name	Product name	Product name
Feature				
Speed				
Guarantee				
Quality standard				
Benefits				
Ease of use				
Speed of deployment				
Price (RRP)				

Your future European customer needs to be able to see the benefits of switching to your product. They also need to find it easy to change. It needs to be perceived as a low-risk decision. That is what I call the **cost of switching**.

Articulate the process of switching to your product in two dimensions: the risk and the advantages. The lower the risk and the higher the advantages, the lower the cost of switching you will get. I've provided an example in the following table.

Risks and advantages of switching

Perceived risk involved in buying your product	Advantage for your customer if they buy your product
As a buyer of this new product, implementing or buying this new product may involve some risk such as: 'It will take a lot of time to stop using our current product and switch to this new product. I need to re-train the entire department to start using the product. I'm not sure they are going to like it; they are reluctant to change.' 'This product is new to the market and does not have a lot of credentials; it's hard to demonstrate to my manager that it is safe to implement in our company.' 'What if I am the only one to buy this new product in the market? And it fails? That would look very bad.' 'We have been using our current product for 20 years and it has been working fine; why should we change for a product that we are unsure of?'	*As a customer, this product will enable me to:* 'This new product will help us generate additional revenue that we are not capturing today.' 'With this product we are going to solve the major quality issues we have encountered on the production line in the past months.' 'This new product will help us save money, because it is going to help us lower our inventory.' 'With this product I can confidently show that we are compliant. We will be ready in case of an audit at any time.'
Prepare your strategy and arguments to minimise each perceived risk.	*Articulate well each advantage. It's important to be able to articulate in euros if you can. Each advantage must be measurable.*

The cost of switching

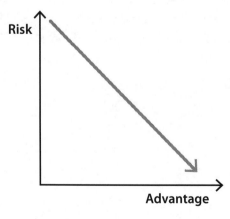

If your product enables your customer to generate more revenue and it's low risk for her to buy, then the cost of switching to your product will be low, and the return on investment will justify the purchase.

Recommended retail price list

Now it's time to formalise your European price list. It will be part of the information you will share with potential customers or partners in the market validation, so get it ready now.

Here are practical tips to formalise it. It must:

- be a single price list for the entire European market

- be in euros

- include an expiration date

- exclude VAT, if you deal in a B2B environment, to make your life easier, as VAT rates may slightly differ from European country to European country

- be public

- not include any special rates or conditions; any special discounts or rates must be kept in a separate document.

Any price increase must be notified to customers 90 days prior to the price increase.

Team

In small businesses, the business owner is often the doer and the bottleneck in chief. There are several points to observe when your team is small. Because of the limited time available for the business owner it's important to make sure that European customers still receive the attention they deserve. You need to create trust with them at the start when it comes to being responsive and delivering on your promises. The business owner, even with all good intentions, may be caught in so many different things he may lose sight of the response time to European customers.

If only one person in the team is interacting with European leads and customers and it's the business owner, you run the risk of being seen as a micro-business. You really need your business to look bigger than what you really are. The reality is, no very large corporate will want to work with very small businesses.

To counteract this issue, involve everyone in your team from day one, even if it's a small team. You may also add to everyone's job descriptions that it is part of their responsibility to provide excellent customer service to European customers, and that any European customer enquiry must be treated with the highest level of priority – even if their level of English in not great! Everybody in the business must be involved in the mission-critical exercise that is export!

Here is how you can get everyone involved:

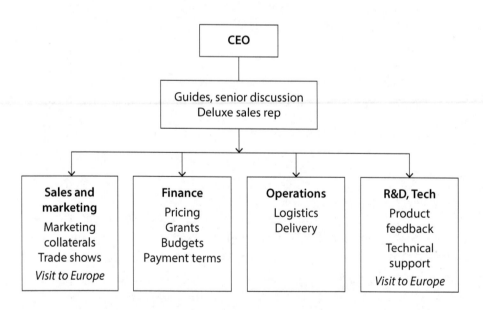

Customers

Building a track record

Your product must be validated by the market. Having buying customers, even just a few, is critical to your success in Europe. A potential European customer will ask: 'Who are your customers in your domestic market?'

If you don't have customers in your home market, Europeans will wonder why you were not able to convince local customers. But if you can demonstrate a strong track record in your domestic market, it will build your credibility in the eyes of a potential European buyer.

Ideal customer profile

Knowing your ideal customer profile before you venture into the European market will save you a lot of time. And time is precious for small businesses; the faster you get results the better for your business. The fastest way to enter the European market successfully is to know your best customers really well. It means you have a very good idea of who your customers are. You know which industry they come from and what typical issues they face. Most importantly, you know how your solution or product can help them solve their problems.

Following is a table to fill in to help you define your ideal customer profile.

Your ideal customer profile

Describe your ideal customer	Answers
Size Number of employees	
Size Revenue	
Industry Industry sub-segment	
What do they do Description of activities	
Contact department Relevant departments at your clients	
Contact person profile Client decision makers – who are they? Job titles, responsibilities, etc.	
Territory coverage Are they typically regional, national, European, global?	
Examples of clients Can you give us company names?	
Value proposition What problem do you solve for this profile of clients?	
Products sold to them Which products do you typically sell to them?	

Value proposition

Before you start contacting potential European customers you need to formalise your value proposition. By going through the exercise of your differentiators and the cost of switching, you should now be able to summarise in a sentence what your value proposition is.

Focus on your ideal customer profile and think about the largest value you bring to this customer. If, for example, I talk about us at Exportia, our biggest value is that we can take small businesses to their first million euros in sales within two to three years.

Think about the problem you solve for your clients and what they most love about your solution or product. You can articulate your value proposition around the three following items:

- Problem: the major issue your customer faces
- Solution: how you help them solve it
- Outcome: the result they get

Step 2: Market Validation

What is Market Validation?

In the Exportia methodology, once we have assessed that your business is ready to export to Europe, we then validate that there is potential in the European market for your business.

The way we do this is that we help you select the top two European countries you should focus on. It is often tricky for small businesses to know where to start in Europe. The choice of the best European country for your business is critical; it will accelerate your success.

In the Market Validation phase, the remaining three of the Seven Export Pillars are addressed:

- Marketing
- Sales channels
- Country.

Once the top two countries are selected, we map out a long list of potential channel partners or distributors in both countries.

We also identify, in some cases, key potential end-users in both countries.

The objective of the market validation is not to sell. It is to gain feedback about the potential of your product or service in the market. It is very important to understand this very clearly. At the initial stages, you need feedback. If you start to sell straight away, your European contacts will close up and will ask you to go away. You need that feedback, and if you just ask for their opinion it's much easier to obtain, and it is less threatening.

People love to share their opinions as experts. You will get a lot out of this stage.

What I also would like to repeat here is that it's important for small businesses to first establish themselves with distributors. In the initial stages, it does mitigate risk for your business.

I have already explained this in the channel section (chapter 4). Let me summarise here the main advantages of having distributors:

- no need to set up a subsidiary in Europe

- hiring European employees too soon is risky; you don't need to if you have a distribution network

- you get fast and cost-effective access to your distributors' sales force; your business gets to cover much more ground and faster

- you get faster access to a large, existing customer base, thanks to your distributors or channel partners.

What do you need to have ready before you start?

Marketing

You need marketing collateral:

- a company profile

- a product brochure

- a case study.

Sales channels

Ideal channel profile

Use this template to define your ideal European distributor/channel partner profile.

European distributor/channel partner profile

Partner profile criteria	Answers
Type What type of channel are they? • wholesaler • channel partner (IT, software, cloud) • distributor • reseller • online shop. Are they selling to distributors or to end-users?	
Size In terms of revenue and number of employees	
Their clients' profiles Which industries and types of clients should they already sell to?	
Commercialisation channels They should: • be pure online • have an extensive sales force • respond to tenders • have a catalogue.	
Salesforce size Number of sales representatives	
Sales team profile Profile of their sales representatives. Any specific technical or industry skills?	

Partner profile criteria	Answers
Breadth of offering Breadth of catalogue range; how many products or solutions do your successful channel partners typically sell?	
Aftersales/technical support Do you expect them to conduct some technical support? Aftersales service? What technical skills do they need?	
Consulting/service/advice capabilities Should your partner have the capability to provide advice or services that would help sell your solution?	
Competitors' products Which competitors' brands do they typically sell?	
Complementary products Which complementary brands or products have a good alignment with your brand positioning?	
Successful distributors/channel partners List the websites of your most successful partners with that profile	
Products sold to them Which products do you typically sell to them?	

A distribution strategy

How many distributors do you need, and what margin should they have as a starting point? This is some of the information you want to have clear in your mind before you start. Go back to chapter 4, where I describe the five stages of establishing European distribution effectively. The market validation is not the time when you actively engage with distributors. It is the time when you ask for feedback. This will also help you prepare the responses to questions your potential distributors may have.

European past interest

Have you had any previous interest in your product or solution coming from Europe? Have you had any European enquiries? Maybe your business has had European customers in the past? This will be useful background information as you go through the market validation process.

Ideal customer profile

Check out chapter 2, Customers – I describe there how you define you ideal customer profile. This is a very important profile. Go on and retrieve what you have completed in this template so far; this is a key element to help you get started with your market validation.

Researching

You know by now that I am very structured and I like to articulate things in processes. I think it's easier to convey and train people how to do a market validation in three stages.

First there is a research phase, then a strategy phase. In fact, your research will enable you to formalise a strategy: your top two countries and your targets in terms of distribution partner and key target customers.

Then, to bulletproof your approach you are going to test it. This is when you ask for feedback from the targeted channels and key target customers.

Once you have done that you will know what you may need to change.

Let's consider the research phase now. The overall objective is to assess if you stand a chance of successfully entering the European market.

Customer research

It's one of the most important elements in your strategy: which profile of customer are you going to target? This is like the heart of the strategy.

First, have a look at your track record. Which customers are your best customers? To determine your ideal customer profile, you need to focus on the customers that get the most from your product. For which customers do you solve the biggest problems? And which customers have the money to pay for your product? It's important you focus on your favourite customers, the ones who don't discuss price.

Once you picture that profile of customers you can fill in the template below. You may have two different categories of ideal customer profiles; that will be fine. It's important you focus on your very best customers though.

Profile of your ideal European client

Describe your ideal customer	Answers
Government or private organisation?	
Size	
Budget or turnover	
Description of activities/roles	
Type of industry/specialty	
Organisational structure/relevant departments	
Who are their clients/their target audience?	

Describe your ideal customer	Answers
Territory coverage (regional, national, multinational)	
Profile and examples of clients you have already sold products to. Provide names. Which products have you sold to them? List them.	
Who are the client decision makers? Job titles, responsibilities, etc.	
Other comments	

Then start to identify key European customers that match this profile. Focus on the top 10 if you can. If your ideal customer profile is a small business, you may find it hard. Let's say you target plumbers. It will be hard to identify the top 10 plumbers in Europe! However, you may want to find out at the European level which European country has the most plumbers, and where they are the most sophisticated for example, if that is relevant to you.

Country research

It's important for your business to make a rational decision when it comes to your top two European countries. We all know it's not about the holiday destination, it's not about a country that speaks English, it's not about family roots. Don't we? It's all about business and sales. I think we all agree on that.

That's why your business needs to focus on the top two European countries that will have the most potential. It is critical to define your selection criteria and to give each of them a weight. Choosing a country that holds good potential will save you time, and consequently money.

Here I have outlined examples of potential criteria. This does not mean that they would be your criteria; these examples will just give you ideas on how to formulate yours.

First, you define your criteria:

- **Ideal customer profile.** This criteria is applicable to any business. If you look back at your ideal customer profile you will find there your definition criteria. For example, you may have created a profile outlining typically multinational companies that are in the chemical industry. You would have maybe detailed a sub-industry. So your first criteria is a country that holds an important chemical industry.

- **Complementary/competing products.** Let's take another criteria; this one may also be applicable to you. Clients of ours often tell us when we go through this exercise: 'Well, if this technology is widely adopted, then we have more chances to sell.' It's often the case, in the tech sector, that you realise your product is often used in conjunction with another product. Or your clients often use a particular product or solution, and this product has a nice alignment with yours. This product may complement your offer. That is why we call them 'complementary products'. If this is your case, your criteria will be to select a country where this product or technology is well established.

  Another way to look at this is looking at the presence of competing products. If your strategy is to tackle and win market share over a competitor, you may want to target a country where this competitor is well established.

- **Pain.** Let's now look at the one called 'pain'. My years in sales at IBM taught me that selling is about finding the customer pain. Your product, particularly in B2B, should solve a customer problem. So it may be important to you that the country you select encounters this type of problem. For example, our clients in the medical sector often tell us that countries that would have encountered specific issues related to public health would create the best environment for them to be heard.

- **Leads.** Sometimes it may happen that your business may have received incoming enquiries from Europe. Or you may have had European customers at some stage but this may have gone cold. If this is the case, it would be useful to collect this information and check which European country they came from. It's very useful information to check if any particular European country emerges. Alternatively, you can also check Google analytics. Are there any particular clients looking at your website?

- **Market size.** This goes hand in hand with your ideal customer profile. However, here we look at the market size, which is the market size for your product. You may be able to find these statistics publicly or you may buy a market study. That's a useful way to look at your market.

- **Regulatory incentive.** One basic requirement for your product to be successful is to make sure that it is approved by the local regulatory bodies. For example, the medical sector is a classic example where some technologies may or may not be approved. If you are lucky, a local regulatory group may recommend your type of technology – that would help a lot.

  In addition, in the green technology sector for example, what we often look for are government subsidies. Several European countries are encouraging investment in green technologies to enable them to meet their carbon emission reduction target. If this is relevant for you, find out which European countries have established such a scheme.

- **Any other criteria?** Have another think; what else? What other criteria is relevant to your business and would enable you to determine that this given European country is a good one for your business?

- **Give each criteria a weight.** For you to determine your selection, you need to define a weight for each criteria; that is, which ones are more important for you.

Criteria	Description	Weight
1		2
2		1
3		4
4		3

Selecting your top two countries

Once you have defined your criteria and your weight for each criteria, it's time to look for the information that will substantiate each criteria.

First, do some broad pan-European searches on your criteria. The objective is to understand which European country emerges. You can have comprehensive market studies done, if you can afford them. They will give you a Europe-wide overview. We usually do without.

Checking the European Union's initiatives is a great way to know which pain is encountered most by which European country.[1] The European Union conducts initiatives and funds projects that solve important issues for the Union. Finding if you can benefit from one of these projects is really helpful to know, and will allow you to trigger the attention of a potential customer faster. You can check which European country is involved in which initiatives. That will give you a lot of important information.

Free and very reliable information is also provided on the European Union statistic website Eurostat.[2]

But my favourite source of information is to simply ask around! I like to target opinion leaders and ask them what they think about a product or technology. I know it sounds very simple, but it's extremely efficient. I will repeat myself here, but what I always find amazing is that people who are really experts in their field are often happy to share their views. It happens all the time.

---

1   https://ec.europa.eu/commission/index_en
2   https://ec.europa.eu/eurostat

All the information you need about competing products and complementary products is easy to find online.

Then it's time to record all the data that will enable you to make your decision and formulate your strategy. This is how we do it:

Criteria	Country 1	Country 2	Country 3	Country 4	Weight
1	*Description*	*Description*	*Description*	*Description*	2
Score	*3*	*2*	*1*	*4*	
2	*Description*	*Description*	*Description*	*Description*	1
Score	*1*	*2*	*3*	*4*	
3	*Description*	*Description*	*Description*	*Description*	4
Score	*2*	*4*	*3*	*1*	
4	*Description*	*Description*	*Description*	*Description*	3
Score	*1*	*3*	*1*	*2*	
Total	18	31	20	22	

Selection outcome:

Top 2 countries
Country 2
Country 4

Researching your sales channels in your top two countries

I mentioned in chapter 4 I have a five-step framework to work successfully with channel partners and distributors. Here it is:

1. Profile

2. Select

3. Engage

4. Activate

5. Manage

Here in this Market Validation process, we focus on the first two steps only: Profile and Select.

Start with profiling the right partner for your business. I have detailed all the elements and the questions you should ask earlier in this chapter. Try to stick to only one partner profile at a time; focus on the profile that has been the most successful for your business in the past.

'How do you search for sales channels or distributors?' is a question that I often get during my workshops. Well, there are many ways to do that. The first thing my team does is to look at exhibitors at trade shows that are in a client's target industry. Then we check the tenders that would have been won by different distributors. We also check which distributors our competitors and peers in our industry are using in the top two countries we are targeting. But the best way is to ask end-users with your ideal customer profile which distributor they buy from. We tend to do that more down the track – it's harder during the market validation.

Researching your key target end-users

Using your ideal customer profile, identify the companies in your top two countries you would like to target. The objective here again is to collect feedback and not to sell.

Search for these companies and identify a contact person with the job role you need. Ideally, at the Market Validation stage you would talk to one or two companies in each of your top two countries.

To find these companies is pretty straightforward; you can do internet searches for the top 10 companies in the industries you target. You can then find the people you need on professional social networks. You can also use annual reports and company websites.

Researching key opinion leaders

This may or not apply to your industry. In the medical sector, it's very common to target a key opinion leader (KOL). It is usually a doctor or a professor who has published in your topic of interest. They are also probably involved in industry associations.

* * *

Once you have identified the countries, companies and people you want to target and the contact people in the companies, you should add the following elements to support your strategy:

- ideal customer profile
- ideal channel profile
- RRP price list
- distributor price list.

Testing

The objective of testing is to obtain feedback about your product or solution from the people you identified during your research. You are also checking if they could be possible future leads, or whether they could be potential customers or channel partners.

Prepare a worksheet to collect feedback, like the one shown on the next page.

Test worksheet

	Call notes	Outcome	OK to be contacted in near future?
Distributors/Channel partner			
Distributor 1			
Contact person 1 Ph E-mail			
Contact person 2 Ph E-mail			
Distributor 2			
Contact person 1 Ph E-mail			
Contact person 2 Ph E-mail			
...			
Client			
Company 1			
Contact person 1 Ph E-mail			
Contact person 2 Ph E-mail			
Company 2			
Contact person 1 Ph E-mail			
Contact person 2 Ph E-mail			
...			
KOL			
Contact person 1 Ph E-mail			
Contact person 2 Ph E-mail			

Here are the steps to follow to contact the relevant people during your testing.

1. Contact

- Focus on the right contact person.
- Have ready your product brochure, case study, and company profile.

2. Ask for feedback

Do not try to sell anything at this stage! Just ask the people you contact for their opinion.

> Dear [XXX],
>
> I am in charge of preparing the entry to the [French/German/Italian] market for my company XYZ.
>
> The product is/does/provides …
>
> The product value add is …
>
> The product credentials are [award-winning, recognition, important clients] …
>
> We are now gathering feedback about the suitability of the product to the [French/German/Italian] market.
>
> In that context, we would like to have your feedback as a [major/renowned/respected] player in our industry.
>
> I have attached a brochure, case study, and company profile for your perusal.
>
> Would it be okay to schedule a 30-minute call with you to have your feedback?

As a tip, I'd like to recommend you also pause your market validation project in the middle of the interviews. Let's say you have interviewed five distributors out of ten. Have a think on how to refine your approach to make it more efficient for the next five companies.

And another tip: once you have had the call with the person to gather their feedback, don't forget to ask them if they would be okay for you to contact them at a later stage, once you are ready to enter the market. You are preparing your next move here. If you can, you can also give them an indicative time.

3. Formalise feedback

Once you have done the round of calls and collected as much feedback as you can, it's time to reflect on the outcome. What we do at Exportia is we look back on how many candidates we had on our list, and the outcome for each.

Country 1		Country 2	
Distributors contacted:	10	Distributors contacted:	10
Positive feedback:	5	Positive feedback:	2
Negative feedback:	2	Negative feedback:	5
No response:	3	No response:	3
Focus on country 1			

If we have at least one positive feedback from one distributor or channel partner, we usually like to consider that there is an interest in the market. The same for a major customer, if let's say a major end-user like a multinational or a large hospital has provided positive feedback. Then we would definitely push through to the next stage.

Then the decision I usually like to make is, which country are we going to focus on? If there is a country that has shown more interest than another country then it is worthwhile focusing on this country. Small businesses have limited resources, and you want to invest your time, energy and resources in the country that has the biggest appetite for your product or solution. This is what the market validation is all about.

It's easier to create traction in a smaller territory rather than in several countries at a time, unless you have plenty of time and money to invest!

If you did not get to talk to anyone, you have not received any feedback, or found it hard to get through, your approach was not sharp enough and you need to review what you are doing. You need to understand that these companies are highly solicited, and Europe is a competitive market. You need to go the extra mile.

Sometimes it may just be that you have not been clear enough. Also it is worth having your intro e-mail translated into the local language to facilitate comprehension; you have to realise that non-native speakers often feel embarrassed talking in English. Make it easy for them to grasp what you are about and what your request is.

If you received negative feedback, are you targeting the right person? Sometimes, it all comes down to talking to the right person.

Remember to take negative feedback as an opportunity to work on the product positioning, and on the product itself. Have you presented the value add the right way? Was it a question of clarity in articulating your unique selling proposition?

Feedback enables you to sharpen your strategy and your pitch, and will allow you to take action to increase your chances of entering the market successfully.

4. Formalise next steps

Once you have done your round of calls and analysed the feedback, formalise your next steps. Usually, you should be focusing on the country that has shown the most interest in your product. And you would have to start organising face-to-face meetings with potential clients, sales channels and key opinion leaders.

I also advise you to check with them which conferences or trade shows they are visiting or exhibiting at this year. You need to start preparing a lead-generation campaign, and in Europe the best way is shows and conferences. Add this element to your plan using the Seven Export Pillars.

Country	Clients	Product	Marketing	Team	Dashboard	Channels
Country of focus	Initial leads Ideal customer profile	Focus product Unique selling proposition Product feedback	Trade show identified Marketing collateral	Team members involved in the business	First year sales target or number of leads target Budget your expenses	Initial channel partner of focus Channel value proposition

Step 3: Lead Generation

From leads to conversion: a push and pull mechanism

In the Market Validation phase, you have validated the interest of potential sales channels or distributors. They seem to be interested. You also possibly have initial leads with potential customers. Then it's time to accelerate things and get you to your first sales.

This will be achieved with two actions that must happen simultaneously:

1. You will need to create leads; this is what I call a 'push'.
2. You will need to secure your distribution channels; this is what I call a 'pull'.

These two actions are interlinked. You will secure and motivate your distributor by bringing leads to the table. You will be able to turn leads into sales thanks to your local partner or distributor who will make the transaction happen for you; they are your channel to the market.

Your objectives for the Lead-Generation phase are the following:

- to sign a test, or a trial, or to close your first sale
- find your anchor client
- sign up your first distributor.

Lead creation

Let's start with lead generation. This is your starting point. You will need to create leads, and to convert that list into your first trial, test or whatever call to action you have defined.

Define your call to action

You need to define a low-commitment action to offer to a prospective client. It needs to be an easy decision to make for a new potential client. It can be a trial for a fee or for free. It is usually limited in time.

You may define your call to action as:

- a proof of concept:
  - you will set up the parameters to the proof of concept
  - you define what success looks like at the end of the proof of concept
- a free sample
- a trial.

Preparing your approach

Take small steps with prospective clients. If they don't know your company, you need to demonstrate your value to them. The way to do that is to first offer a meeting to present your product. In that meeting you then propose a call to action.

You may need some extra support to convince your prospect to make a decision. You could for example offer for them to talk to one of your customers, or visit one of your customer's sites.

Generate leads

Where to find leads? And how to go about it?

This is the first question that comes to us at Exportia. Leads need to correspond to your ideal customer profile and be from the top one or two industries you will focus on.

Buy a list

One way to find a list of leads is to buy it from a reliable source. European privacy laws are quite stringent, so make sure you are authorised to market to that list.

When buying a list, the quality of the leads can be quite poor and this is quite normal. You will need to go through each list of leads and validate each contact; make sure the person is still at the right job position. And also make your way through to the right contact.

Make your own list

When I look back at European lead-generation projects we have conducted, we usually conduct very targeted campaigns; the outcome we want is – say – 20 highly qualified and warm leads. This is a good number of initial leads for our clients that are starting in the European market. These conversations we have with prospective clients are part of a learning exercise.

We usually use the ideal customer profile to then identify the top 50 company names in that industry and then identify the right contact person with the job role we are looking for. We get our initial list of companies from multiple sources: Google searches, local industry associations, database subscriptions, trade show lists of exhibitors in that industry. In several countries there are public lists of companies based on their industry sectors and company numbers.

Then we usually combine it with a list of inactive leads that our clients may have given to us. And then we start the good old cold-calling process. In my view, this is pure enjoyment! When you start from scratch there is no better way to learn about your industry in Europe: you need to have conversations with your target customers.

Lead-generation campaign

Once you have a beautifully polished list of leads, you are ready to start! Here is your checklist of the things you need to get started with your lead-generation campaign:

- your leads list
- a company profile
- a product brochure
- a case study or referee
- your value proposition
- your call to action.

It's important for you to clearly state the objective of your call; for example, get a meeting or schedule a webcall. It's also crucial to be concise in your presentation of your business and your value proposition. You need to also leave time for your prospective client to share their feedback and to understand what makes them tick.

Put your detective hat on and find out your customer's pain. Where does it hurt? How do you help cure their pain? These are the main questions you need to respond to for the specific industry and clients you will target first in Europe.

Why do you need to find that out? Well, it's fine to have a great product, software or solution, but you need to know how badly your prospective clients need your product. If there is no strong incentive for them to buy now then it will be hard for you to get your first leads. Doing lead generation is great as a fact-finding exercise, but what you are really interested in is finding out who is ready to buy – and now!

The best way for you to sell as soon as possible is to find a customer who has an immediate problem to solve. The other dimension to find out is how big the problem is. Is your solution going to significantly improve their life or not? If you can solve an immediate, very big problem, then you are going to be very successful, and quite rapidly.

To qualify your leads you need to assess how big their pain is and how quickly they are able to do something about it. This will allow you to rate your leads. Give your leads three ratings: high, medium, low. Focus on the high-priority leads and make sure you turn them into customers. You are better off focusing on a limited number of high-priority leads rather than spreading yourself too thinly.

Participating in a conference or a trade show

One of the best ways to generate leads is to attend a conference and a trade show. At Exportia, we use these events to launch our clients' products and generate our initial list.

Europeans still organise major shows where, as a newcomer in the European market, you will have the opportunity to meet potential customers and partners. This is a great tool to get a quick overview of a market, and it's available to anyone.

I strongly recommend you exhibit at large international shows, as well as at smaller and more targeted conferences. In some instances, smaller conferences may provide a better targeted audience.

We like to get a hundred leads from a large international trade show. This can be a great starting point in a market and can provide you with your first list. In a smaller conference, you can expect to obtain thirty well-qualified leads. Realistically, even if you just convert one lead into a sale or even just a trial, you are in!

Remember GDPR

Don't forget to observe the General Data Protection Regulation (GDPR) – ask people for their consent on the spot at your stand to upload them to your database and to send them a regular newsletter. You need their formal consent. Prepare a simple form and ask them to tick the boxes.

Here is a quick summary of things to remember about trade shows and conferences:

- They are still the most efficient way to generate leads for a newcomer in a market.

- Choose carefully:
  - Which conferences/shows do your customers visit? Or exhibit at?
  - Which conferences/shows do your distributors exhibit at? (Exhibit! Not only visit.)

- Always comply with GDPR.

Two ways to exhibit

Exhibiting on a distributor's stand can be a good option when you start in a market. It's cheaper and it is a good way to evaluate if this is the right show for your business. However, it gives you less control and you won't get the full benefits of a exhibiting under your own name.

Exhibiting yourself versus being on your distributor's stand

Exhibiting	On distributor's stand
You are open for business for any partners, customer	You are limited to your distributor
You build your brand	Lower brand exposure
Significant investment	Cost effective
Your keep control of the leads	You may not have the ability to capture all the leads You don't own the leads

Keep your deadlines in mind

I have outlined for you below a timeline to prepare your key milestones in the preparation of your show presence. It's important not to miss these deadlines or you may miss the registration dates.

Preparation timeline prior to show day[1]

One year	Six months	Three months
• Large shows: register! • For smaller shows/ conferences, ask for the registration dates • Get info to apply for an award • Get information to speak/ submit an abstract	• Prepare booth • Create a professional display • First time? Keep it lean	Lead-generation campaign: • Set up meeting planning • Translate your brochures • Book the scanner machine to save time at the show

---

1 Go back to chapter 5, Marketing for more detailed planning.

Secret tip number 1: Make new friends

Once you are at the show, it's important of course to talk to potential customers and distributors. This should be your focus.

However, I will share with you a bit of my secret recipe for success: it's called 'making new friends'. It's fun, and when you are in sales, that is why you do this job. It's one of the ways I use to quickly immerse myself in a new industry.

At a conference or at a trade show, there is always down time. That down time is usually the last afternoon of the show. Or it can be early morning prior to the opening of the show, or just before the show ends and the visitors have already started to go home. It can also be during conference time. Or sometimes, let's be honest, the attendance may not be great. It can also be during dinners or functions that are run by the show organisers.

When there is down time, I go around and introduce myself to my peers. I usually go to the booth of companies that have a complementary product to the one I'm selling. I go to their booth and meet their sales directors or their key account managers. First, it is really interesting to meet new people; they live and breathe in your industry and sometimes they have done so for years. I tell them that we are entering the market; I give them our credentials ('We are well established in Australia, in the US, some of our clients are … ') to build trust. I explain to them clearly that we are entering the market and that I may see them again. I tell them what we have in mind for the market, and I cross check that my information is correct.

You need to, of course, be aligned with that person. They need to play in the same field; they need to be non-competing. You need to trust that person, so ask them about their background.

From these conversations, so many positive outcomes have happened. I have made actual new business friends. I have also been given lead contact details – this happens regularly. This is really powerful when you start from zero. I'm also getting a bit more insight on distributors. It's a really powerful diligence tool: is that distributor reliable? How is their negotiation style? Who's who in the zoo?

Secret tip number 2: Secure a meeting on the spot

My experience is that it's much harder to secure a meeting once the show is finished rather than during the show. For very warm leads that I meet during the show, I usually like to secure a meeting with them while I talk to them on the stand. You avoid the back-and-forth e-mails and the time difference issue if you are far away from Europe. This is a great way to get it done.

You will feel the reaction from your leads. They might say: 'Wait before scheduling a meeting; I need such and such information', or, 'I need to check with our technical department first'. Whatever the outcome is, it's interesting for you to know what the steps are to get a meeting: in our examples: 1) type of information needed, 2) what does the technical department need to check?

So worst-case scenario, you don't get the meeting but you get more information on their decision process and it helps you prepare to secure your meeting.

Secret tip number 3: A fast follow up after the show

After the show it's critical that you do your follow ups quickly. It's critical not to lose momentum with these leads. Give your prospective clients the information they requested – the brochure or any other document they asked for – and prepare for the next steps.

At the same time, you can update your leads list in your CRM and set up their preferences. Have they agreed to receive a newsletter or not?

Then set up your meetings.

After your *push* (lead creation) now is the time to *pull*

The concept of push and pull

Once you have established your list of leads and you have started to have sales conversations with them, it is a good time to work in collaboration with your potential new distributors.

Once you have generated a few leads, find out from your prospective customers who they are buying from. Who are their distributors or partners? It will be easier for you to generate the interest of a potential distributor or partner if you have triggered the interest of their clients. What I really like to do is to target a large potential customer; the larger the better. That large customer is certainly one of the favourite customers of your potential distributor. The best way to win that distributor is to win that customer over.

This is the most powerful tool you have as a newcomer in the market. Customer is king. If an important client wants your product, you have your way in with a distributor.

When the time comes to discuss price with your potential new customer, don't forget to only mention list price. Let your distributor make the offer and have the margin they need. Work as a team with your distributor's sales representative in charge of this customer and show her how to sell the product. Let your distributor do the proposal and the final contractual arrangement.

Not only do you now have a new distributor, but with that distributor's sales representative that you have just worked with, you also now have two more feet on the ground to sell your product.

Engage new distributors

In parallel, you continue your conversation with the potential distributors that you approached in the market validation phase or at a trade show. Focus on the ones that showed the most interest. Test their appetite for your product and assess if they are likely to move fast.

Initially, you want to set yourself up in the best conditions possible in the market. To do that, make sure you inform the distributors you are talking to several distributors or partners. Let them know that you are going through an evaluation process.

As I mentioned in chapter 4, Sales channels, my preference is not to grant exclusivity to any distributor. I like my clients to be in control. Giving distribution to only one distributor restricts your market. It also can make your distributor lazy. It makes them feel comfortable, and it does not give them any hurry to push your product. Having at least two distributors will create a nice dynamic and will keep them on their toes.

Think about having a mix of small and large distributors. You can get early wins with smaller distributors. They usually are agile and fast. Your larger distributor will be slower to get started. They tend to be slow to take on new products and they make decisions at a slower pace.

Have your negotiating position ready

Have your trading terms and your margin ready before you approach a distributor. In the Market Validation phase you would have already given some indication on your list price. Now is the time to share with them their conditions of purchase.

In the table opposite is an example of how to formalise your distributor offer. Or you may want to outline your offer in an e-mail instead; you can use the fields as a checklist to make sure you don't miss anything.

Ref.	Description	HS commodity codes	Minimum order quantity	Ex-works unit price, [CITY], [COUNTRY]	Total
Product category 1					
Product category 2					
Product category 3					

Terms and conditions

Prices effective 1 January 2020 and valid until 31 March 2020
All prices are in euros and do not include value sales tax
All prices are ex-works from our facility in [CITY, COUNTRY]
Payment terms are 30 days from end of month. Note: [YOUR COMPANY NAME] reserves the right to change the payment terms for late payment.

Delivery times

For orders of [X] units or less, [YOUR COMPANY NAME] will have the order ready for dispatch within 7-10 days from receipt of the purchase order.
For orders over this amount, [YOUR COMPANY NAME] will confirm the order time.
Shipping time from [COUNTRY] is usually x to y days per air freight and x to y weeks per seafreight.

When you start to engage with a potential new distributor, don't forget that terms and negotiations should be based on performance. It would be wise to start with a less favourable position for your distributor with the option to offer better conditions once the distributor has performed well.

You can tell your potential new distributor what they need to achieve to obtain better conditions. For example, you may tell them that if they achieve a target of 100,000 euros in the first year, you can improve the conditions.

In the case of larger distributors, they may impose on you their agreement. You can go over this topic and refresh your memory by reviewing chapter 4.

In summary, my advice is to first ask for an agreement in English, or get it translated into your own language. Usually large distributors are used to having overseas suppliers and will have a translation ready. I would recommend you get legal advice if you are unsure of some of the clauses. Watch out for clauses that mention requirements that are difficult to meet for a small business. For example, some penalties in case of late delivery are too risky for a small business to accept. Don't hesitate to say no to anything you find unfair or something you cannot guarantee because it's not in your control (for example, shipping). The reality is that you are a small business to them and you are not so important in their eyes. You are only a minimal share of their business, and therefore they sometimes are okay to let go of some clauses.

A few legal obligations to be mindful of:

- any new pricing or price increases are to be communicated in writing 90 days prior to coming into place.

- you cannot impose on your distributors their selling price.

The outcome

The desired outcome of the Lead-Generation phase is to secure your first sales. In parallel, that should have enabled you to secure an active distributor. This active distributor can now go on and generate more sales for you.

It's now time for you to scale your business to your first million euros in sales and beyond.

Step 4: Scale

The objective of the Scale stage is really to place your business in a position to generate its first million euros in sales and go beyond. Your ability to scale your business will mainly depend on your capacity to finance further expansion, and on your ability to structure your European systems for them to further grow with local teams.

It's crucial for this process to be staged. Our experience with Australian companies in Europe demonstrates that it usually happens in three stages:

1. From initial sales to several hundred thousand, say 500,000 euros: you **S**ecure your anchor clients and **C**onvert leads into sales.

2. From 500,000 euros to one million euros: **A**ccelerate sales.

3. From one million euros: **LE**verage.

Each stage requires you to have a specific focus. It's important not to go too fast and to secure every step along the way.

Scale stage 1: From initial sales to 500,000 euros (reinforcing your European foundations)

After you have completed your Lead-Generation phase you should have a basis for further expansion. You should have one or two distributors in place. You should also have well-established customers, what I call anchor clients. By now, your distributors would have generated sales. Now it's key to do more of the same! Basically, you are securing your position and reinforcing your European foundations.

215

You are focusing on one European country only, the country where you have the most leads and where you have managed to engage at least one distributor to sign your first sale.

It's also important that you focus only on the distributors you have just engaged in the Lead-Generation phase. Don't spread your resources too thinly.

Securing anchor clients and converting leads

Securing anchor clients is your first priority

Your first clients in the market, your anchor clients, are going to be your point of reference for the rest of the market. You need to reinforce your support to them to make sure you establish a long-term relationship. For that they need to have a very high satisfaction level.

They also need to feel that they have a prime relationship with you, that you take into account their feedback and you always listen. These clients are really important as they are often very enthusiastic about your product. They are great advocates for you in the market.

One way to drive customer loyalty is to provide excellent customer service. What I personally like about anchor client relationships is that they go beyond the normal scope of 'client–supplier'. Here are the characteristics of anchor clients that I often came across:

- they are often part of a large organisation, a multinational
- they are active in their industry and involved in steering committees or industry associations
- they open doors and refer your solution to their peers
- they are proud to have 'found' you, and to be an early adopter.

Converting more leads into sales

The Lead-Generation phase will enable you to secure your first sales. You should also have developed a list of leads to work on. Keep at them; regularly follow up with them.

The conversion of these leads will happen with the help of your distributors. Here is how you can share the activity between you and your distributors to increase your turnover with them.

Who			Does what	In order to		
Your company	Together +	Channel partner	Activity	Care for anchor client	Generate leads	Support partners
X	X	X	Visit customers	X	X	
X	X	X	Exhibit at trade shows		X	X
X		X	Technical support and advice	X	X	X
X			Train how to sell			X
X		X	Train end-users	X		
		X	Prepare proposal	X	X	
		X	Sign contract	X	X	
X	X	X	Customer service	X	X	
X			Get a referral from	X		
X			Leads management	X		X

Activate your sales channels

For a while, you will focus on your key distributors. It's important for you to fully activate them and and manage them. This step is often overlooked by companies. The mistake they make is that they sign the distributor up and they wait for the sales to come. Unfortunately, this is very rare.

To generate your first sales with your distributors you need to activate them. You need to show them the way to being successful with your product. The magic formula is:

$$\text{Distributor} + \text{Leads} = \text{Sales}$$

In addition, it's important to convey to them the best way to sell your product. For example, you want to make sure that they target the right contact person. In some instances it may be the technical department, rather than purchasing. There might also be a few things to qualify that the client is the right client for your product. For example, we have a client in the safety industry. For them, what is critical is that the company has set a high priority on compliance. The companies that care about compliance are typically larger companies. In that case, you need to *train your distributors' sales teams* in that perspective. In your sales training you will explain to them who the best customers are and what their profiles are. During sales training, I usually like to *identify my champions*. And I plan to conduct customer visits with them. I will show them how to sell a couple of times, for them to be comfortable enough to do it on their own.

At the end of the sales training, you will need to deliver tools for your distributors' sales team to be comfortable with selling. These *sales tools* will help them build confidence with your product. It can simply be a brochure, a video or a demonstration kit. It's particularly important for your champions to have everything they need to sell.

Finally, it's important that you *send them leads*. For example, what we typically do with my team is once we have built a list of leads or have generated leads at a conference or a trade show, we hand it over to the new distributor we have just secured. It gives them a place to start. It builds confidence that this new product will bring business to them. They will take you seriously. It's really a key success factor to be able to support them with leads. Then they will start to do the same for you and to refer leads to you.

The side benefit to handing over leads will be that you are now in a position to manage your leads and create a regular reporting structure to check with them how these leads are progressing.

Key success factors to activate a sales channel

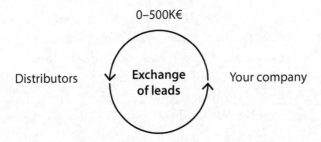

Don't forget to *report back to the distributor's management* on your progress; share with them the leads you have handed over. I would recommend you regularly follow up with management on the progress of the leads. If you have handed over leads and nothing is done about them, it gives you the ability to renegotiate a contract, or detect an issue. You can openly discuss it with management and solve the issue.

Be a regular at trade shows

Continue to exhibit at the same trade shows you exhibited at in previous years. You will see your relationships with your leads and clients reinforced by that presence. The discussions will open up a bit more every time. Regularity will give you a way to build your credibility in the market.

Companies that did not have a chance to stop at your booth the previous years might stop this year. It's amazing how things change year after year.

Hiring sales agents

While you grow your sales, you will need some extra support. Depending on the country you are focusing on, establishing a network of sales agents is a great way to get the help you need. I have seen sales agents more commonly for manufactured products, rather than in software. However, you may find other types of contractors that could work.

In some European countries they are more common than others. I have found them over the years mainly in the UK, France, Italy, Spain, Belgium, Austria, Switzerland and Germany. Depending on the industry, they may or may not have a good reputation. So, you need to check with your distributors or channel partners if they are aware of any sales agents, and what they think about them. In the German market, for example, in a specific industry I did not find great sales agents. The distributors did not think highly of them. I struggled to implement a network of sales agents, and had to hire staff instead.

The idea of sales agents is to increase your reach and have country-wide coverage of salespeople talking about your product all day long. They work in tandem with your distributor sales team, and make sure you stay top of mind. They usually know their region inside out and can introduce your brand to nice clients of theirs.

Have a look back at chapter 6 to refresh your memory on sales agents.

Scale stage 2: From 500,000 to a million euros in sales (expansion)

Lead generation and lead conversion – again!

In order to generate several hundred thousand euros, you have to focus on your first one or two distributors in one country. This gives you the focus and the time to make it happen. Then it is time to further expand and prepare your next round of growth.

In the country where you are currently active, you continue to generate sales and pursue your sales activities as follows:

Who			Does what	In order to		
Your company	Together +	Channel partner	Activity	Care for anchor client	Generate leads	Support partners
X	X	X	Visit customers	X	X	
X	X	X	Exhibit at trade shows		X	X
X			Technical support and advice	X	X	X
X			Train how to sell			X
X			Train end-users	X		
		X	Prepare proposal	X	X	
		X	Sign contract	X	X	
X	X	X	Customer service	X	X	
X			Get a referral from	X		
X			Leads management	X		X

In addition, it's time to conquer additional accounts. It might mean focusing on an additional industry, it might be by way of launching a new product, or it could be a service.

Time to appoint one or two new distributors or channel partners

In your country of focus, you can expand your coverage further by appointing one or two new distributors. Are you missing out on deals because you don't have enough distributors?

One powerful way to trigger the interest of a new distributor is to talk to one of their favourite clients. Once you have convinced their favourite client to buy, you ask them to introduce you to their contact at their distributor. Once the introductions are made, you are in a better position to talk to that distributor, in comparison with starting cold. Explain to the distributor that their client wants to buy, and that you are happy to work with them to make the deal happen. You might make a new friend!

Of course, as you secure the transaction, don't forget to still complete the steps to get high-performing distributors. Activation is a key part. They need to have stock; you need to train their sales team. That will enable you to identify champions and generate additional leads.

Talking to leads and asking them who they buy from is not the only way to go. In parallel, if you have conducted a market validation as per our methodology you should already have mapped out potential distributors or channel partners that match your channel profile. This is also a good time to have another look at that list and detect a potential candidate.

Selecting a new country

Starting to establish your presence in a new country always takes time. Once you have some success in a country and have nice European clients that you can mention as references, it will be much easier to start in an additional European country.

Where to next?

If you are not clear on which European country to go to next, I recommend you go back to step 2: Market Validation in our method. You may already know which country to focus on according to the research you would have done in the Market Validation.

Once you are active in Europe it will be easier to do that selection using the simple Exportia Country Selection process we use in a Market Validation phase. Define your criteria of selection and check which European country best meets these criteria.

Once you have picked your next country, map out the potential distribution partners in that country. Now you have more reasons to contact them. It will be easier as you have more European clients. That will open doors for you. As per a market validation, gather their feedback first.

Once these potential new distributors have given you their positive feedback, it's time for you to generate leads for them. Here we go again; you are off to generate leads in that new country. Implement another Lead-Generation phase.

Leverage your wins in Europe

In your expansion, you want to fast track your sales using and leveraging your European wins:

- **Anchor clients:** Get friendly introductions from your anchor clients: do they have colleagues in the country you are targeting? Your clients are very likely to have branches in many European countries, if not all.

- **Channels:** Refine your initial channel partner profile; has anything changed? Have you learnt anything you should implement for the next European country?

- **Marketing:** Build a library of European case studies. Exhibit at European trade shows that are international; it will drive new leads from additional countries.

- **Dashboards:** Keep an eye on your leads and on how they convert. Work with your distributors to prioritise these leads and convert them into sales. This can be done in your customer relationship management system. A very simple approach we always implement on behalf of our clients is to have a monthly call with distributors to follow up on their leads and check how we can support them. On a simple level you can have a leads list per distributor in a spreadsheet.

Country 1	Country 2: New!
Channel: + 1 **Marketing:** Trade shows and conferences **Team:** Sales agents; Time to detect potential future employees! **Customers:** Reinforce your ties with your customers with excellent customer service **Dashboards:** Lead management	Market validation Lead generation

In this fashion you expand by focusing on one country at a time. After the second country has achieved a million and above, you can start on the next country.

Companies that have greater resources may also proceed in this way, but they may also have the financial resources to target additional countries at the one time. Sometimes it's easier to add an additional smaller country in parallel to this approach, but only if you can afford it. If you are stretched for resources then keep your focus on one country at a time.

Once you have reached a million euros in sales, it's time to structure your presence in Europe.

Scale stage 3: Structure (setting up the machine: one million euros and beyond)

When you start to reach above a million euros in sales, continued success comes down to setting up the structure of your business properly. Each of the Seven Export Pillars is impacted. However, the critical one to scale your business will be *team*. Yes, the people that are going to take the business to the next level need to be carefully selected. They are critical to your business.

Hiring your first team members in Europe

It's all about the team at this stage. You need to start recruiting people in Europe. It's exciting – and it can be scary as well!

The first profiles that small businesses often hire in Europe are either a technical profile to support customers or a salesperson. Sometimes you can combine both profiles to have a technical–sales profile.

The type of people you need to hire

What's critical is hiring people who are independent enough to work remotely, away from HQ. However, they need to have the right set of communication skills to stay in sync with your head quarters.

It requires them to be happy working on their own a lot of the time. Their autonomy clearly needs to be a criteria in your recruitment.

The other trait I like to add when I recruit is I like to assess their ability to reliably report back and communicate. It's important for a person who will work away from the rest of the team to be open about any issue they have.

In line with this, they also need to abide by the rules. If you have a system, procedures, or if you are using a CRM for example, you need to make sure they use your systems and they also comply with your guidelines. Things go wrong when the first European employees feel they are on their own and they have to implement new systems – they end up becoming completely desynchronised from HQ. Or your new European employee – having no day-to-day guidance – gets lost and is not sure what to do. That's even worse.

They also need to be accepting of the fact that it won't be perfect. Your small business is starting in the European market, so they won't have a team of a hundred people to meet their every need. I have interviewed candidates who have worked their whole career for large multinationals. The risk for a small business with this type of profile is they won't be able to adjust to the small business constraints. In small business, if you don't have the right brochure, you create it. If you need something you will do it yourself, rather than relying on a team to make it happen for you.

When it comes to the first salesperson I recruit for our clients, I often have a few candidates in mind that I invite to apply. I usually have met them at trade shows or while I'm networking with my peers who are working for non-competing brands.

There is that typical distinction about salespeople: you have the farmers and the hunters. For your first sales recruit, you definitely want to focus on recruiting a hunter. You need a person who is able to build business from scratch and will knock on every door and travel far and wide to prospect.

A farmer would be much more comfortable building relationships and growing business from an existing portfolio of customers. This is not what you need straight away.

In the interview, I really focus on digging around their ability to create new leads. The candidates need to convince me with clear examples, and referees need to support this.

Of course, in many European countries you have the option of developing a broad sales agent network. They are independent operators. They have a portfolio of products that are aligned to yours. They visit daily the customers and distributors you deal with or want to deal with. This is a good option too.

When it comes to marketing, I would recommend you hire marketing agencies based on what you need. In the initial stages, you don't need a full-time person. You can manage your marketing needs from HQ. This keeps your costs down and also enables you to maintain consistency in your messages.

One of the first types of profiles that my clients hire is a technical support person. Our clients are software developers or manufacturers of technical products. They often need local technical support to be able to provide excellent service to their brand new European clients. Once you have started selling, you need to ensure the delivery and implementation of your product is a success. That's when your technical person can guide, train and support your customer all the way.

Taking care of your customers will guarantee you long-term relationships with them. They need a local person to look after them. It needs to be a local who speaks their language; it goes without saying!

Creating your pool of candidates

I like to have a couple of candidates I have come to like and trust over the years of developing the market for my clients. I really like to make new friends, and at a quiet show or before a show starts, I make sure I introduce myself to my peers. Of course, you are not mingling with your competitors, even though it's fine to meet and greet them. You want to create a network of people that you can potentially work with down the track. The great thing about that is you can really see over the years how they operate. It's very easy to check how they are perceived by the market.

We have also used a recruitment agency to be able to reach additional candidates. It gives you more chances, especially in employment markets that are tight, like the German market. It's really important to have as many candidates as possible.

Understanding your employer obligations

Before you hire, get legal advice. Have a clear understanding of the legal implications of hiring, and know your responsibilities in terms of regulations, tax and social benefits. It's important for you to know what's involved; for example, you need to be across the typical length of a trial period. You need to make it as long as you possibly can to give you the opportunity to move away from a candidate if she does not do the job well.

You also need to take into account a candidate's notice period at their current job. It can be up to three months. This can be negotiated with the employer, but sometimes if this is a good employee, they won't want to let him go until the last minute.

Each European country has their own employment and workplace laws. Unfortunately, the European Union has not con-solidated this part of the law yet. So, a local lawyer who is qualified in the given country will usually give you much better advice than a lawyer based in another country. Get a local employment lawyer to brief you about your legal obligations, and to draft an employment contract. It's important for them to brief you on the dismissal process as well. Know where you stand before you start employing.

Working with and managing your European team members

Maintain consistency

There are a few things to consider when managing a European team from a head office outside Europe. Remember that they are the face of your business in Europe, so they really need to be consistent with the rest of the business. Give them clear guidelines about what is expected from them and how they have to deliver each outcome.

I think it's quite important to maintain consistency for small businesses growing internationally, especially with your marketing. One common error is for European teams to reinvent the wheel and create additional marketing material for themselves, whereas that brochure may already exist and just need to be translated. In addition, you don't want to find that your German or Italian team has come up with a whole different message that is at the opposite of your core message. And you won't even know because you don't speak German nor Italian!

That would not be great. However, it's easy to keep control of your message and have a single English 'reference' brochure that can then be translated into many different languages.

It's easy to keep control of your marketing message. The same applies to your branding. You just need branding guidelines for everyone in your international team to use.

Maintain regular contact

One of the most important points is to maintain regular contact. Sometimes it might seem hard with time differences and distance. But really you want to be able to take the pulse of your team on a regular basis on the phone, conference calls and through regular visits.

Be culturally sensitive

Every European country has its own culture that you will get to know as you work with Europeans. One of the most important qualities to have when you are dealing with different European cultures is humility. You have to be open and humble to understand what is really going on and learn from it. Remember that Europeans should be managed differently depending on their cultural background.

When you grow your team in Europe, cultural sensitivity becomes even more important. There are a few important situations where cultural sensitivity is particularly required:

- **When deciding who manages who – which nationality manages which nationality?** If you appoint a manager from a more individual-focused culture (Dutch, Scandinavian) to manage someone from a group-focused culture (Spanish, Italian), you will need to contemplate having some cross-cultural training.

- **Providing feedback to your team.** When it's time to evaluate the performance of your team, it's critical for you to understand how people like to be given feedback. I'm French, and I have several nationalities in my team. The best way to manage cultural sensitivity around feedback has been to ask them how they would like feedback to be provided.

- **Team projects.** If you have to run a group project, be also mindful of the different cultures in the group and the impact on group dynamics. Remind participants about their cultural differences so they can take care during their interactions.

- **Long-term versus short-term goals.** Airbus is a true pan-European company. It is co-owned by the French Lagardère and the German Daimler. During an interview, the CEO said that when appointing a team to manage projects, he would always give the long-term research project to the Germans and he would always give the project with tight deadlines to the French; somehow they will manage it and will be able

229

to cope with the pressure. However, putting pressure on a German team would never provide good results.

Provide impeccable support

Make a point to support your European team the best way you can. My experience is that teams can start to feel demotivated when they feel they are on their own, or it takes ages to receive responses to their technical requests. Hearing their concern and doing something about it – such as establishing a time to dig into it and establishing a plan to solve it – boosts team morale.

You want everybody to be focused on sales and not on little problems. If little problems multiply, the frustration of your European team will grow and it will affect their performance. Tackle issues as they arise, even if you just talk about it, find that it's not a high priority and decide together to park it for a while. At least if you have gone through the process with your team, they will feel heard. They can also understand that you may have other priorities to tackle first.

Keep your European team accountable with KPIs

Key performance indicators are widely used in Europe; nothing new here. It's a great way to motivate sales teams, and it's a great tool to motivate a new team member who starts in a new territory. Of course, sales targets are perfectly suitable for sales teams. However, very often for small businesses expanding in new territories, it's good to set key performance indicators on activities that will enable revenue. It's a great way to encourage your team member because sometimes sales won't happen overnight, so you need to reward them on the activities that are going to generate revenue. For example, if the priority is to set up new distributors then the number of distributors signed up and fully trained might be an indicator. It might be the number of new qualified leads with a certain profile of company. For more senior positions, it might be about them recruiting new team members.

The most important point about key performance indicators is really about tracking them. I like quarterly KPIs; it keeps a team member focused on what she should achieve. It's easier not to forget. And what is also really important is to keep checking in on how that indicator is going for your team member on a regular basis. And to check with your team member if she needs help.

When is a good time to set up a subsidiary in Europe?

There is a point when it's wise to set up a subsidiary in Europe. I would say when you start to plan to hire your first European team member then it is a good time to set it up. You need to abide by the local laws. And get advice from a local accountant and a local lawyer to get support.

I know some of you may be tempted to look at fiscally advantageous locations to establish your European HQ, such as Switzerland or Luxembourg, but times are changing. European tax offices are now having a closer look at companies with commercial activities in their country and with a headquarter located in countries with much more favourable tax regimens.

Several European Union members have requested that large technology companies be taxed based on the revenue they generate in each country, and not based on where they book their profit.[1] Many large technology companies have optimised their tax by being based in Ireland, where the fiscal regimen is very favourable, whereas their largest shares of revenue are generated in larger economies, such as Germany, France, Italy or Spain. I am not a fiscal adviser, and cannot advise on this matter. However, when companies ask me where they should set up their European offices, I tend to propose they evaluate several options before they make their decision:

- **Where most of your turnover comes from:** I think it makes sense to locate your European headquarters in the European country where you generate most of your revenue.

  Often, small businesses that are new to the European market start to generate revenue in a specific country first. This

---

1   https://techcrunch.com/2017/09/11/france-germany-spain-italy-call-for-turnover-tax-for-tech-giants/

country is often where you are going to recruit most of your team members, so it makes sense to locate your HQ there. This is where your team is, and where your largest clients would potentially be.

If you have a team spread across many different countries then the location of your team is not a relevant criteria. Then you may want to look at other criteria. Keep reading!

- **Where you set up your logistics platform:** If you ship goods to the European Union, and have your logistics platform based in the Netherlands or in Belgium because of their large port infrastructure, that can be a logical next step for you to localise there.

- **Where the fiscal and government incentives are the most favourable:** Let's not be naïve here; of course European countries have developed programs to attract foreign investment. They run programs to support a business when establishing in Europe. They offer a range of services for free. I have often seen programs to promote the registration of intellectual property in the country. Another very strong incentive for the country is of course job creation.

    In preparation for Brexit, European capitals have been very active in attracting foreign investment away from London and to set up in their capital.

- **Where it's easy for you to communicate with the local authorities:** One day I was helping one of my Australian customers make a decision on the location of their European head office. We talked to government representatives from the UK, France, Germany, the Netherlands, and Belgium. I was quite disappointed to see that the only country that presented us documents that were not in English was France. I was a bit embarrassed for my customer; even though she was very lovely and open-minded, she had not learnt French overnight.

So yes, the ability to access authorities in English is a good thing. You don't need to use interpreters, there are no translation costs, and there is a reduced level of misunderstanding too. The Netherlands is a really good location for that.

- **Where the location of your HQ can be useful for your brand image:** Well, I guess if you are in fashion you would want to be established in Paris, wouldn't you? We don't play in consumer goods, but one of my clients has a medical device, and I can already see that being a reputable company with a German subsidiary would give them instant credibility. It would also give them access to the community of German healthcare companies. For the rest of Europe it will look good to have their European head office in Germany.

- **In the European Union!** Of course, you want to create your subsidiary in the European Union. For the accounting, legal, and customs aspects it will make your life so much easier! In addition, your team members can freely circulate and work in the European Union member countries. You will get an Intra-Community VAT Number that will allow you to easily collect and deduct the payment of VAT.

Can you have an HQ in an EU country and your team members based throughout the EU? Yes you can, and this is one of the major advantages of having your European HQ in the European Union.

Customer

As you grow your business in the European market, there are two major challenges that I see our clients are facing:

1. maintaining excellent customer service to keep your customers happy

2. accelerating the deployment of projects Europe-wide, and leveraging European synergies.

I find that these two points are key for you to further expand your business in Europe in a sustainable manner. And they are not easy to establish. Let me explain.

Maintaining excellent customer service to keep your customers happy

As you grow your business in Europe, it will offer new opportunities for your business, as well as new challenges. You will have to structure your customer service to make sure you maintain good long-term relationships with your European customers. Your European customer satisfaction is paramount; it's your repeat business. It is cheaper to grow a business with current customers than acquiring new customers.

It's time to organise great customer service. This comes with challenges as well!

Maintaining consistency and accuracy

As you grow, you will train your sales team to be able to respond to administrative and technical enquiries that are fairly basic. But then, your sales team will have questions for you. And they will have more and more of them as your business grows.

For administrative enquiries related to delivery times and invoices, we find that usually the people in charge of logistics and operations and those in charge of the accounts should rapidly be introduced to distributors and large customers. It is better for the sales team not to have to manage too many administrative tasks, otherwise they start to get distracted from selling. They should be informed only when it's important for them to know.

A bigger challenge is when you grow your team, they have to deliver the right information and the right advice that is accurate and consistent with the message delivered by HQ. I don't see any better way to do this than regular product trainings for the team.

With our clients we have organised this through webinars. It works really well. The teams are quite receptive to that. It is cheap to run too. I have run technical trainings for sales teams in Europe –the presentation was delivered by a product manager in English and my team and I were here to facilitate in case there was a need for a translation. One of your European team members who speaks good English can be that helper for the rest of the team. Nowadays, webinar services often also provide interpreters. That is a great service. But I would recommend somebody trained to be able to assist with technical translations.

Have clear guidelines on what type of typical questions a salesperson should be able to respond to and when it's time to ask for some help. You don't want to have a sales team that starts to give technical advice they are not sure of, or for which they have not been trained.

It's very useful to have a dedicated person at HQ who can be that go-to person, who is always at the office – somebody who is not travelling. They can build their experience about typical technical enquiries that European customers have, and then train others on this. Their role will be to respond to technical enquiries from the sales team. The European sales team processes the request from the end customer, and has been trained to ask the right questions. They can then bring as much context as possible to the technical support team.

It's important to train your sales team on bringing specific information. Every salesperson needs to find out specific information from the customer before they ask a technical question.

Providing a fast response

Ultimately, customers buy a product or software, but they also buy the service along with it. And they may decide to switch to a competitor's product if they feel they have received bad service. So, fast response is key.

The first easy step is to simply inform them that you have received their request and that you are looking after it. This is so important for a European customer; when they have an issue or a question, they can be acknowledged that somebody is currently looking after their enquiry.

This gives you a bit of breathing time to look at the request, prioritise it and prepare your response.

There are a lot of software platforms that can help you track customer enquiries; give the customer a reference number and you can run statistics on response times. This is a real challenge for small and medium-sized companies; they often have a limited number of people at HQ who are handling these enquiries.

You know when those trails of long back-and-forth e-mails start to go nowhere? Then it's best to ask your European sales team to organise a conference call with the customer, and they can translate the questions and answers for you. I have found it to be the best way to close customer enquiries that are a bit harder to deal with.

I really like how some of our customers have created online forms for technical questions or issues that capture the context they need to be able to provide a fast response. You can cover 80% of typical enquiries this way. Some of my customers have also used their website to share some technical tips and responses to customers. I do find them to be very useful for sales teams to refer to as well. The use of diagrams and images is a great way to make them explicit. Remember, it's easier to translate when it's not too wordy.

How to respond to customers asking questions in different languages

Some businesses create European phone numbers for which they have recorded voice mailbox messages in different languages. And that allows the business to call a customer back about their issue.

Google Translate does perform quite well nowadays. It saves a lot of time and money to use Google Translate to translate e-mails or documents that do not need to be published. It can be helpful, and quicker than using a translator.

Until you have a local team to handle customer service, you have to find cost-effective ways to provide good customer service.

Accelerating the deployment of projects Europe-wide, and leveraging European synergies

This is what large multinationals and small and medium-size business that are growing internationally do badly. Companies with international presence – whether they are small, medium or large – often perform poorly when it comes to leveraging their European presence across multiple countries.

European countries trade mostly among themselves, thanks to the common EU market. Therefore, as you develop relationships with one multinational organisation in one country, leverage that organisation's ties in other European countries. It's critical to do so to expand quickly.

It is also so much easier to expand into a new country after being introduced by a company that already buys and appreciates your product. You already have a reference point.

Whether you are dealing with a large distributor or a large client end-user of your product, you should ask them for the contact details of their European colleagues. It does help.

As your sales team grows and you start to have more senior team members coming along, it's a good time to start building a team of sales professionals who are able to drive European sales from your key accounts. They are called 'key account managers', and they should ideally have European experience to be able to collect these pan-European contacts, reach out to them, and hand them over to their local colleagues.

Marketing

Once you are generating at least one million euros in sales, you have the means to increase your marketing activities. You now have more cash to be more sophisticated in your marketing.

A yearly calendar of shows

After a few years you will clearly know which European trade shows work for you the best. Usually international customers and distributors visit these shows. It's a good chance for you to run customer activities and plan events around the trade show. The difficulty will be ensuring that everyone will be there the same day! That will be your challenge; to mobilise your customers and sales teams to make it happen.

In addition, you may have national shows. In the countries where you have the majority of your turnover, you may decide to exhibit. These are also important. Sometimes, I find them a bit quieter than the European shows that are more international. So, pick the ones that have really good value.

Local, specialised shows are cheap and usually provide well-qualified leads. Make sure you have identified these shows, and plan for a few of them throughout the year. They are more local but they really are efficient. It's easier to visit your local show.

Well prepared trade shows are still the best way to create a significant number of leads. They also generate some nice opportunities to create content for your social media presence.

Now that you know your favourite shows, plan for your yearly marketing calendar.

Lobbying influencers

This is an activity that I particularly love doing and have been quite successful with. It does really take the business of my clients to another level. Once your business is established in a specific country, it's important for your brand and your products to be known by influencers. It takes a while to build a network of influencers in the market, but it is really important to be seen as a major player.

The influencers can be so different from industry to industry. In the medical sector, the influencers are the doctors and professors that are going to publish about your product. For one of my customers – an automotive aftermarket accessories manufacturer – we lobbied the car manufacturers, even though we would not sell to them.

I would recommend at this level of turnover (greater than one million euros) you start lobbying activities if you have not done so in the past.

Dashboard above one million euros

In that above one million euros in sales bracket, you are monitoring your sales and marketing budget closely and have a more structured sales reporting system. You may have to report to a board or a management team on your plans and on your progress.

Sales and marketing budgeting and forecasting

Marketing costs

It now becomes critical for you to collect information for your budget from the European region and to include this in your global yearly sales and marketing plan. And there is a logical step here for budgeting: cost of exhibiting, booth layout, accommodation of your team, printing of brochures and banners are all part of it. You may add a budget for social media advertising and ads in magazines as well. It is good to support sales this way.

I would also add some budget for samples and demonstration kits for your sales team.

Sales team expansion

It may be time to recruit more salespeople! If you want to add another salesperson, add these recruitment costs and plan for a recruitment agency. Often what also happens is that your existing team members have access to their own network. Still, I think it's good practice to budget for some recruitment costs.

In addition to that, you may be able to expand your network of sales agents. So, you may want to anticipate 5% to 10% of your sales for sales commissions.

Sales forecasts

European sales teams need to prepare for you their sales forecasts for the year. What sales target do they wish to achieve with the allocated budget?

I think it's very important to encourage sales teams to project their minimum forecasts, their feasible figure, and the figure that they would really love to achieve. Then it's important for them to be able to regularly report against it, ideally on a monthly basis.

Leads and customer management

With a turnover about one million euros, you have to know your leads and customers! And you need to have a way to hold, manage and nurture your customer details. Of course, your CRM activities need to be GDPR compliant!

It is all the more critical to have up-to-date customer records as you may start to have some of your European team leave you. It's been a few years now that you are active in the European market. If someone from your sales team leaves you, you need to ensure that the recordkeeping is spotless and that you are not at risk of losing some precious customer contacts.

In addition, you will get a better pulse on your European sales if you know how many leads you have and at what stages they are at. It's also very important to know which lead is managed by which distributor. And CRMs are great for you to track your distributor activity.

Product above one million euros

Introducing new products regularly

Keeping the momentum will require your business to launch new products regularly. Distributors and key customers will be happy to see that you are in the market to stay, and that you keep innovating. It will comfort them in their decision to work with you.

Europe is a competitive market, and your competitors are watching you. With one of my customers we worked several years on cracking a specific market. It took a lot of education for the market to accept the technology. Because they were the first ones in that market, they were able to achieve the largest volumes. It was nice to see these sales, but my client and I already knew they needed to bring a new product to the market very soon. Their competitors were quickly catching up.

New products reinvigorate your extended sales team, whether they are your own, your sales agents or your distributor's representatives. It's always motivating for a salesperson to visit their customer to present a new product. And distributors love the fact that they are able to present an innovation to their clients. Instead of having to present a product that everyone else is also selling, they love to be able to differentiate themselves this way.

What is really excellent as well is to be able to bring in modifications and improvements to your product that your European customers have asked for. It really builds trust and loyalty. Taking into account their feedback makes them feel heard, and they will love your product even more for that.

Logistics platforms

It might be the time to also think about having a logistics platform based in Europe. I am an advocate of having distributors stock your product as much as possible. However, I recognise that it may be an issue for some particular products. For one of my customers, for example, we could not use distributors to sell to key accounts because the key accounts in question were only buying direct from suppliers and in large volumes.

My client had to organise a logistical platform quite early for that specific reason. Typically third-party providers are great for small businesses. And considering locations close to ports such as the Netherlands or Belgium are good options. Then it really depends where your market is and where you are dispatching to.

Channels above one million euros

Your sales channels are in full swing above one million euros. You should have a nice network of distributors or channel partners. Now the critical issue is to keep them motivated and at the same time maximise your coverage.

This is the fifth step I covered in chapter 4: Sales channels. After having generated one million euros in sales, you now have to manage closely your current distributors, making sure they keep growing.

At the same time, it's important to keep expanding your network. Some channel partners or distributors may be stronger in one industry and quite weak in another one. So make sure you reach your full potential. It's very common after a while working in a market to realise that your distributors don't cover some key customers you would like to target. So keep expanding your distribution network to keep growing your sales.

Another key element to consider is to establish sales targets for your distributors on a yearly basis. And make sure that you monitor their progress on a quarterly basis.

Summary of the Seven Pillars

Seven Pillars	0	500,000 euros	1,000,000 euros
Your focus	Secure and convert	Accelerate	Establish your structure
Channels	Focus on 1 or 2 Activate sales channels	Add 2 sales channels	Distribution program and management KPIs
Country	1 focus country	1 focus country Select an additional country	Expand to more countries Set up a EU company
Customer	Lead generation Create anchor clients Leads conversion	Lead generation Customer service	Customer service Pan-European synergies, key account management
Marketing	Trade shows	Trade shows	Yearly marketing calendar Lobby influencers More marketing euros on advertising
Team	Hire sales agents	Sale agents	Hire employees
Product	Focus on core products	Focus on core products New product launches	Focus on core products New product launches
Dashboard	Leads management	Leads management Forecast	Leads and opportunity management Forecast Yearly sales and marketing budget

CONCLUSION

You have made it all this way. Congratulations on joining me on this journey to take your business to its first million euros in sales.

What's really important is to embrace the step-by-step process and to start implementing now. Go ahead and follow the process for your business.

In this book we have gone through an entire system to take you from zero sales to one million euros in sales and beyond. Here is the summary of our 4-step methodology to generate one million euros in sales. As a guide along your journey, I have also summarised for you the major actions to conduct at different stages of your journey in Europe:

1. Export Readiness Diagnostic: Get ready to export to Europe

- Compliance
- IP protection
- Can you fund it?
- Customers

2. Market Validation: Determine your potential in Europe

- Your top two EU countries
- Get feedback from 30 partners and key target customers
- Decide on your unique country of focus

3. Lead Generation: Generate your first sales

- Trials, proof of concepts

- First sales

- Lead generation

- Secured and engaged sales channels

- Exhibit at trade show or a conference to generate leads

4. Scale: Grow your sales to one million euros and beyond

- 0 to 500,000 euros: one (or two) countries max: Secure and convert

- 500,000 to 1,000,000 euros: Accelerate sales

- Greater than 1,000,000 euros: Structure your presence in Europe

In going through this 4-step methodology we have debunked a few myths along the way.

Just for fun, let's test your knowledge, now that you are familiar with the 4 steps to generate your first million euros in sales:

Please respond with TRUE or FALSE:

1. You need to set up a subsidiary in Europe to be able to grow your European sales: TRUE / FALSE

2. To succeed in Europe the first step is to hire a senior salesperson based in Europe: TRUE / FALSE

3. Signing up a Europe-wide distributor is a fast entry into the European market: TRUE / FALSE

4. Having exclusive distributors is the best way to get fast sales and secure your business: TRUE / FALSE

5. The best way to cover the European market is to start with the UK, because of the language, and then you expand into continental Europe from there: TRUE / FALSE

Check your answers – they should be: 1: False; 2: False; 3: False; 4: False; 5: False.

Congratulations if you successfully passed this test. Now is the time to go ahead and implement our method piece by piece and build your own European empire. You know that Rome was not built in a day, and you will keep in mind that this is a long-term process, and you will have to invest significant time, money and resources. But the potential of the European market is massive, and this is quite a safe market for your business if you are well prepared.

Now it's time to take your first step. This is easy: take the test on the Export Readiness Diagnostic Tool: http://diagnostic.exportia.com.au/7pillar/

Once you have your report, check with me if you are eligible for a 45-minute session with me to debrief on your report.

Good luck!
Christelle Damiens

APPENDIX A | COUNTRY PROFILES

I have prepared several country profiles with pieces of information that I find useful to know for small businesses in the European market. As mentioned earlier, small businesses often make the mistake of rushing into one specific country, without having undertaken a selection process. These profiles aim at highlighting interesting facts such as the multinationals that originate from each country, the share of SMEs in their economy, and the number of hospitals. Each European country has a different profile.

Germany		Source
Sectors	Four sectors dominate industry in Germany: the automotive, mechanical engineering, chemical and electrical industries. Mechanical engineering is characterised by small and medium-sized enterprises.	1
Population	81,197,537	2
Large multinationals	Volkswagen, Daimler, BMW (all automotive), BASF (chemical) and Siemens (electrical)	1
Share of SMEs	2,408,540	3, 4
Hospitals	3084	5
Other information	No. 1 European economy	

France		Source
Sectors	Industry represents more than 17% of GDP and employs a fifth of the active workforce. The key industrial sectors in France are telecommunications, electronics, automobile, aerospace and weapons. The tertiary sector represents around 70% of the French GDP and employs more than three-quarters of the active workforce. France is the leading tourist destination in the world with nearly 87 million foreign visitors in 2017.	9
Population	66,415,161	2
Large multinationals	LVMH, L'Oreal, Total, Airbus group, Sanofi	8
Share of SMEs	2,908,814	3, 4
Hospitals	3046	5
Other information	France is the European leader for the number of patent applications filed in the healthcare sector (CSIS, 2016)	7

United Kingdom		Source
Sectors	In 2017 the services industry (including retail, accommodation, business administration and finance) contributed £1.4 trillion in economic output, 79% of total UK economic output. Manufacturing output was £188 billion, 10% of total output. The construction sector's output was £116 billion, 6% of total output.	10
Population	64,875,165	2
Large multinationals	BP, Prudential, HSBC, Tesco, Aviva, Legal&General, Lloyds	11
Share of SMEs	1,940,947	3, 4
Hospitals	207 clinical commissioning groups; 135 acute non-specialist trusts (including 84 foundation trusts)	12
Other information	Date planned to leave the EU is January 2020	

Italy		Source
Sectors	The services sector accounts for almost three-quarters of total GDP and employs around 65% of the country's total employed people. Within the service sector, the most important contributors are the wholesale, retail sales and transportation sectors.

Industry accounts for a quarter of Italy's total production and employs around 30% of the total workforce. Manufacturing is the most important sub-sector within the industry sector. The country's manufacturing is specialised in high-quality goods and is mainly run by small and medium-sized enterprises. Most of them are family-owned enterprises.

Agriculture contributes the remaining share of total GDP and it employs around 4% of the total workforce. | 13 |
Population	60,795,612	2
Large multinationals	ENI, ENEL, UniCedit Group, Intesa Sanpaolo, Telecom Italia	14
Share of SMEs	3,683,127	3, 4
Hospitals	1,063	5
Other information	Italy has been ranked 2nd by Forbes for its shadow economy	15

Spain		Source
Sectors	Agriculture contributes to around 2.6% of Spanish GDP and employs 4% of the workforce (World Bank, 2017). The industrial sector accounts for 21.6% of GDP and gives employment to 19.3% of the workforce. Manufacturing is the most important industry as it accounts for around 82% of total production (mainly textiles, industrial food processing, iron and steel, naval machines, and engineering). The tertiary sector contributes to 66.4% of GDP, mainly tourism and banking.	17
Population	46,449,565	2
Large multinationals	Banco Santander, Telefónica, Repsol, ACS, Iberdrola	16
Share of SMEs	2,465,540	3, 4
Hospitals	777	5
Other information	The country is the second most popular tourist destination in the world.	17

Poland		Source
Sectors	Agriculture, manufacturing (automotive, shipbuilding, petrochemicals, electronics, electrical machinery), energy, and tourism.	18
Population	38,005,614	2
Large multinationals	PKO Bank Polski, PKN Orlen, PGE, Grupa PZU, KGHM Polska Miedz	19
Share of SMEs	1,606,559	3, 4
Hospitals	1,058	5

Netherlands		Source
Sectors	The top Dutch sectors are defined as: high-tech systems and materials, logistics, energy, agri and food, creative industries, chemicals, horticulture and propagation materials, water, life sciences and health.	20
Population	16,900,726	2
Large multinationals	Philips, ASML, Automotive Campus, ASM international, TOMTOM, Vanderlande Industries, ABN AMRO, ING Group,Rabobank, Aegon, Delta Lloyd, Capgemini, Fujitsu, Oracle, Ahold, Akzo Nobel, Heineken, Royal Dutch Shell, Unilever	21
Share of SMEs	1,092,243	3, 4
Hospitals	545	5
Other information	The Port of Rotterdam is the largest port in Europe	53

Belgium		Source
Sectors	The country's nominal GDP ranks the 25th highest in the world and the 37th highest based on purchasing power parity. Belgium imports most of its semi-finished and raw material goods which are processed and exported as finished goods to different countries around the world. Different industries are found within the country, which includes refining, textiles, chemicals, steel, pharmaceuticals, food processing, electronics, machinery fabrication, and automobiles among others. The service sector accounts for about 74.9% of the country's GDP and agriculture contributes approximately 1% of the GDP.	22
Population	11,258,434	2
Large multinationals	Anheuser-Busch InBev, KBC Group, Ageas, Solvay, Dexia, Belgacom, Banque Nationale de Belgique, Delhaize Group, Colruyt, Umicore, UCB	23
Share of SMEs	602,153	3, 4
Hospitals	174	5
Other information	As explained in the *Brussels Times*: 'Belgium has three official languages, Dutch, French and German, but the country itself is neither bilingual nor trilingual. Nor can you officially be addressed in English. The official language of the Flemish Region is Dutch, while the institutions in the Walloon Region (minus the German-speaking Community) speak French.'	52

Sweden		Source
Sectors	Main industry sectors are: agriculture, forestry, and fishing, resources and power, manufacturing, finance, trade, services, labour and taxation, transportation and telecommunications.	27
Population	9,747,355	2
Large multinationals	Volvo, Electrolux, Ericsson, H&M, IKEA, Spotify, King Digital Entertainment	28
Share of SMEs	686,433	3, 4
Hospitals	81 (2003)	5

Czech Republic		Source
Sectors	The GDP of Czech Republic is US$215.7 billion. The service industry is tops in terms of GDP contribution to the economy of the country at 59.7%, followed by the industrial sector at 37.8%, and finally the agricultural sector at 2.5%. The labor force for these sectors stands at 59.2%, 38%, and 2.8% respectively. There are also great opportunities for investment in nanotechnology, research and development, business support services, life science, cleantech, and the aerospace industry.	24, 25
Population	10,538,275	2
Large multinationals	Komerční banka, Česká spořitelna, ČSOB, UniCredit Bank, Česká pojišťovna, Kooperativa pojišťovna, Škoda Auto car manufacturer, Agrofert Holding, Hyundai Motor Manufacturing Czech, Metrostav and Eurovia CS	26
Share of SMEs	1,001,048	3, 4
Hospitals	255	5
Other information	It's interesting to note that a lot of European and American manufacturers have chosen the Czech Republic to establish manufacturing facilities.	

Portugal		Source
Sectors	This country has a GDP of $205.86 billion that when adjusted for purchasing power parity is equal to $310.651 billion. The majority of the working residents in this country are employed by the services sector (69.1%). This sector is followed by industry (24.5%) and agriculture (2.4%). Within the industry sector, corporations operating in this country tend to produce the following goods: machinery, automotive and ship parts, textiles, refined oil goods, plastics, food products, and beverages.	29
Population	10,374,822	2
Large multinationals	EDP-Energias de Portugal, Galp Energia, Jeronimo Martins, Portugal Telecom, Banco Comercial Português, Banco BPI	30
Share of SMEs	807,183	
Hospitals	225	

Finland		Source
Sectors	Finland excels in the export of technology as well as promotion of start-ups in the information and communications technology, gaming, cleantech, and biotechnology sectors. Other important sectors are: electronics and the electrical industry, machinery and transport, forest industry vehicles, chemical industry, power and water supply, metal products, food industry, metallurgy and mining, publishing and printing, and non-metallic mineral products.	31, 32
Population	5,471,753	2
Large multinationals	Stora Enso, Neste Oil, UPM, Metsäliitto (inc. M-Real), Kesko, Sampo, SOK, Outokumpu, Tamro	32
Share of SMEs	350,000	33
Hospitals	280	5

Switzerland		Source
Sectors	About 80% of industry output is exported, accounting for more than 40% of Switzerland's net visible exports. The output of Switzerland's MEM industry includes machine tools, household goods, and construction plant and specialised microelectronic apparatus.	35
Population	8,605,465	36
Large multinationals	Nestlé, Adecco, UBS, Zurich Financial Services, Credit Suisse, Swatch	34
Share of SMEs	142,775	
Hospitals	281	
Other information	Unsurprisingly for a country with a sophisticated manufacturing industry but few natural resources, foreign trade generates a major share of the GDP. The EU is predictably Switzerland's major trading partner, followed by the US and China. The most important trade goods, both for export and import, are chemicals, machinery and electronics, precision tools, watches, jewellery, agricultural products, vehicles, textiles, leather, rubber and plastic.	34

Austria		Source
Sectors	The most important industries are food and luxury commodities, mechanical engineering and steel construction, chemicals, and vehicle manufacturing.	37
Population	8,576,261	2
Large multinationals	OMV Group, Raiffeisen Bank International, Erste Group Bank, Vienna Insurance Group, Voestalpine, Verbund, Strabag, Uniqa, Andritz, Volksbank, Immofinanz	38
Share of SMEs	322,325	3, 4
Hospitals	271	5
Other information	There is a very strong link between Austrian companies and Eastern Europe. You will often find that Austrian distributors have branches or are very active in Eastern Europe.	

Denmark		Source
Sectors	Health-tech, medical, biotechnologies, pharmacies and hospitals, smart city solutions (IT sector, big data and urban management), design and creative industries, green and clean-tech technologies	39
Population	5,659,715	2
Large multinationals	A.P. Møller-Maersk, Danske Bank, Novo Nordisk, Carlsberg Group, Vestas, TDC A/S, Nokian Tyres, Novozymes, Coloplast, Jyske Bank	40
Share of SMEs	210,726	3, 4
Hospitals	32	41

Norway		Source
Sectors	Major Norway industry sectors span the oil and gas sector which constitutes 25% of the country's GDP, followed by fish farming, fisheries and mineral resources. In addition, Norway is one of the top three seafood-exporting nations worldwide. Around 95% of production is exported. Norway's economic activities include shipping as it has the world's fourth largest fleet. Norwegian industry sectors: agriculture, minerals, petroleum and oil exports.	42
Population	5,258,000	6
Large multinationals	Equinor, Telenor, Norsk Hydro, Yara International, DNB, Orkla Group, Aker Solutions, Storebrand, Gjensidige	43
Share of SMEs	293,403	3, 4
Hospitals	3.8 beds/1,000 population (2015)	50
Other information	In Norway, the average household net-adjusted disposable income per capita is US$35,725 a year, higher than the OECD average of US$33,604 a year.	51

Ireland		Source
Sectors	Gypsum mining processing, food products, pharmaceuticals, rail transportation equipment, glass and crystal.	44
Population	4,628,949	2
Large multinationals	CRH, Development Capital Corporation (now DCC), Smurfit Kappa, Ardagh Glass Sales, Ryanair, Kerry Group, Primark, Total Produce, Musgrave, Kingspan	45
Share of SMEs	243,433	3, 4
Hospitals	81	5

Estonia		Source
Sectors	More than 71% of the Estonian GDP is derived from the service sectors, industrial sectors yield 25% and primary branches (including agriculture) approximately 4% of the overall output.	47
Population	1,313,271	2
Large multinationals	Ericsson Eesti, Tallink Group, Baltic International Trading OÜ, Eesti Energia, Orlen Eesti OÜ, Tallinna Kaubamaja, Neste Eesti, BLTR Grupp, Rimi Eesti Food, Swedbank	46
Share of SMEs	68,124	3, 4
Hospitals	57 (2007)	48
Other information	E-Residency is a unique scheme that enables digital entrepreneurs to start and manage an EU-based company online. Online businesses really need to check this scheme out.	49

1. Source: https://www.deutschland.de/en/topic/business/germanys-industry-the-most-important-facts-and-figures

2. Source: Eurostat; https://europa.eu/european-union/about-eu/figures/living_en#tab-1-0

3. Definition of SMEs in Europe: The European Commission defines SMEs as those enterprises employing fewer than 250 people that have a turnover of less than 50 million euros and/or a balance sheet total of less than 43 million euros. https://ec.europa.eu/eurostat/statistics-explained/index.php/Statistics_on_small_and_medium-sized_enterprises#SME_definition

4. Number of SMEs: https://ec.europa.eu/eurostat/statistics-explained/index.php?title=File:Number_of_enterprises,_turnover_and_persons_employed_and_the_share_of_enterprises_with_fewer_than_250_persons_employed,_2015.png

5. OECD, Number of Hospitals: https://stats.oecd.org/index.aspx?DataSetCode=HEALTH_STAT

6. Eurostat 2017

7. https://www.businessfrance.fr/en/invest-in-France-key-industries

8. Companies in the top of the stock exchange: https://www.boursier.com/indices/composition/cac-40-FR0003500008,FR.html?tri=dcapi

9. https://import-export.societegenerale.fr/en/country/france/market-sectors

10. UK Parliament, Research briefing, 2017: https://researchbriefings.parliament.uk/ResearchBriefing/Summary/CBP-8353

11. Management Today: https://www.managementtoday.co.uk/20-british-companies-worlds-top-500/any-other-business/article/1357359

12. NHS confederation: https://www.nhsconfed.org/resources/key-statistics-on-the-nhs

13. Focus Economics: https://www.focus-economics.com/countries/italy

14. Forbes http://www.economywatch.com/companies/forbes-list/italy.html

15. Forbes: https://www.forbes.com/sites/niallmccarthy/2017/02/09/where-the-worlds-shadow-economies-are-firmly-established-infographic/#c183f85742cc

16. Global database: https://www.globaldatabase.com/top-35-companies-in-spain-by-revenue-in-2017

17. https://www.nordeatrade.com/fi/explore-new-market/spain/economical-context

18. https://industryeurope.com/repo/

19. http://www.economywatch.com/companies/forbes-list/poland.html

20. https://www.cbs.nl/en-gb/background/2017/41/top-sectors-account-for-one-quarter-of-gdp#id=undefined

21. Netherlands Multinationals : https://www.amsterdamtips.com/multinational-companies

22. World Atlas: https://www.worldatlas.com/articles/what-are-the-biggest-industries-in-belgium.html

23. Forbes: https://www.economywatch.com/companies/forbes-list/belgium.html

24. World Atlas: https://www.worldatlas.com/articles/what-are-the-biggest-industries-in-the-czech-republic.html

25. Czech Trade: https://www.businessinfo.cz/en/about-the-czech-republic/economic-information/market-information-sectors-and-products.html

26. Deloitte : https://www2.deloitte.com/cz/en/pages/about-deloitte/articles/cze-tz-ce-top-500.html

27. Britannica: https://www.britannica.com/place/Sweden/Economy

28. Forbes: https://www.forbes.com/sites/kurtbadenhausen/2016/12/21/sweden-heads-the-best-countries-for-business-for-2017/#3dff69aa7ecd

29. World Atlas: https://www.worldatlas.com/articles/the-biggest-industries-in-portugal.html

30. Forbes: https://www.economywatch.com/companies/forbes-list/portugal.html

31. Forbes: https://www.forbes.com/places/finland/

32. https://finland.fi/business-innovation/finnish-industry-constantly-adapting-to-a-changing-world/

33. Statistics in Finland : https://www.stat.fi/til/alyr/2016/alyr_2016_2017-12-21_tie_001_en.html

34. Internations: https://www.internations.org/switzerland-expats/guide/working-in-switzerland-15505/economic-sectors-and-taxes-in-switzerland-2

35. Economy watch: https://www.economywatch.com/world_economy/switzerland/industry-sector-industries.html

36. Swiss: http://worldpopulationreview.com/countries/switzerland-population/

37. https://www.austria.org/economy

38. Economy Watch: https://www.economywatch.com/companies/forbes-list/austria.html

39. https://www.regionh.dk/english/businesses/Business%20Stronghold%20of%20the%20Capital%20Region%20of%20Denmark/The%20Four%20Main%20Business%20Sectors/Pages/The%20Four%20Main%20Business%20Sectors.aspx

40. World Atlas Denmark: https://www.worldatlas.com/articles/largest-danish-companies.html

41. https://www.afr.com/work-and-careers/management/why-denmark-is-reducing-hospitals-while-we-are-building-more-20190219-h1bg9d

42. Economy Watch: https://www.economywatch.com/world_economy/norway/industry-sector-industries.html

43. World Atlas Norway: https://www.worldatlas.com/articles/largest-companies-in-norway.html

44. Economy Watch: https://www.economywatch.com/world_economy/ireland/industry-sector-industries.html

45. Bank of Ireland: https://www.thinkbusiness.ie/articles/the-10-biggest-irish-businesses/

46. https://bnn-news.com/top-estonian-companies-turnover-listed-104916

47. Estonica.org: http://www.estonica.org/en/Economy/General_overview_of_Estonian_economy/Structure_of_the_economy/

48. https://www.ncbi.nlm.nih.gov/books/NBK459022/

49. https://e-resident.gov.ee/

50. https://www.cia.gov/library/publications/the-world-factbook/geos/no.html

51. http://www.oecdbetterlifeindex.org/countries/norway/

52. https://www.brusselstimes.com/all-news/magazine/49791/the-flemish-movement-how-language-shaped-belgium/

53. https://en.wikipedia.org/wiki/Port_of_Rotterdam#targetText=The%20Port%20of%20Rotterdam%20is,by%20Singapore%20and%20then%20Shanghai.

APPENDIX B |
USEFUL TRAVEL COMPANIES

Travel agent	
www.flightcentre.com.au	For Australian businesses, Flight Centre for business has worked great for us. You just need to train your consultant with exactly what you need and she/he will make it happen.
	Provide them with a detailed itinerary and times and days where you want to be and when. Then they can help.
Trains	
www.thetrainline.com	This website is great to book European trains; it's got nice deals that usually your travel agent does not have access to.
	Great to keep control of your carbon footprint. Take the train as much as possible instead of flying.
Car rental	
www.hertz.com	I have used them for many years. I like their loyalty program that allows you to access your car fast and go! Receiving all the invoice via e-mail.
	Also sometimes I need to cancel a reservation and it's really a no brainer, it's very convenient.
www.sixt.com	I mention Sixt here, because non-Europeans may not know this company. This is a German car hire company and they have the best footprint in Germany. Sometimes I use them; my travel agent accesses them when he can not find the right cities or opening hours with Hertz.
Hotels	
www.booking.com	You would know these. No comment in particular.
www.airbnb.com	
www.accorhotels.com	
Planes	
www.edreams.com	There are very good deals.
Airlines direct	You can book directly with the airlines.

A Maya.
Quelle fierté d'être ta maman! Merci.

Thank you to our Exportia past, current and future customers, I wrote this book with you in mind.

Andrew Griffiths, thank you for your mentoring during the entire book process. Your positive voice and your advice have been key to materialising this book.

Thank you to my informal mentors and supporters: Martine Joly and Gordon Kay, you two are a rock-solid inspiration.

Thank you to Michael Hanrahan Publishing for their professionalism.

Thank you to the Exportia team for their ongoing support. I would particularly like to thank Isabell for the initial salary search, Khrystyna for the checks in the IP section and Leo for some of the country statistics search.

Thank you to my partner Nik for the unconditional support in whatever I do and for coping with my frequent travel.

Many thanks to my family and friends for the love, the joy and for keeping me sane.

Free Export Readiness Diagnostic

Are you ready to generate your
first million Euros in sales?

Take the test: diagnostic.exportia.com.au

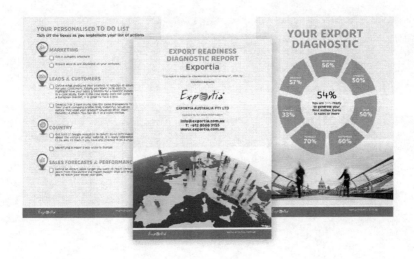

Within 20 minutes, get a diagnostic,
a personalised 'to do list', and a benchmark

You can also read Christelle's first book **Ready, Tech, Go!**

The Definitive Guide to Exporting Australian Technology to Europe available on **Amazon.**

"Christelle Damiens is a true leader in the exporting arena - she's completely across the issues and the opportunities."

Andrew Griffiths

"I really enjoyed Christelle's "Ready Tech Go!" book and found it provided a good framework for businesses to plan international exporting efforts. A few of my students last semester read the book for an extra credit assignment and I am planning on using when teaching global marketing courses in the future."

Jim Blair

Christelle Damiens

Managing Director | Author | Speaker

Christelle Damiens is the Director of **Exportia** - which provides an Outsourced European Sales & Marketing Department to Australian companies.

While working closely with dozens of high-tech Australian companies over the past decade, Christelle has developed a powerful and proven 4-step export methodology. For every client that comes on-board, Exportia number#1 priority is to generate their first million Euros in sales.

Christelle founded Exportia in 2006, shortly after she migrated to Australia from France. She had worked in sales at IBM Paris for six years, but she decided to turn back on her successful corporate career to pursue her passion for international business. With her European sales experience in high-tech environments and ability to communicate fluently in three languages (English, French, German), Christelle decided to dedicate her company to helping Australian small and medium-sized businesses to grow their sales in the European market.

Christelle has an MBA from Edith Cowan University in Perth and a degree in business administration from the École de Management de Normandie. She is also the Author of the Amazon Best Seller "Ready Tech Go! The definitive guide to exporting Australian technology to Europe"

Want to hire Christelle as a Speaker?

For the last 13 years, Christelle has conducted a range of workshops, presentations and keynotes to businesses about exporting, the European market and about her journey as an entrepreneur.

Christelle has created and delivered tailored presentations for a number government departments (New South Wales Premier Cabinet, Ausindustry, the Netherlands Investment Agency) as well as for industry associations (The Export Council of Australia, The Anna Rennie Chapter, the Australian IT Industry Association) and private organisation such as the Key Person of Influence Brand Accelerator and multiple business incubators in Australia and internationally.

Christelle has experience in delivering her presentation in numerous formats from webinars, workshops to keynotes. She places a lot of emphasis in tailoring the content to the audience. She favours interaction with the audience and also likes to provide practical tips, templates and tools.

Christelle can deliver presentations in English, French and German

Book Christelle for your event today

christelle.damiens@exportia.com.au
+61 2 8068 9155

Christelle is able to deliver presentations about a range of topics:

- Export readiness
- Recruiting, managing and motivating European distributors
- Choosing the Right European market for your business
- Exporting technology
- Exporting for small businesses
- Choose the right European market for your business
- Exporting to Europe

- Motivating and managing distributors
- Managing European Sales team
- B2B International sales
- Small businesses and start-ups going global
- Being a woman in international business
- International business travel
- Scaling small business to multi-million euros

"Christelle Damiens is an interesting, relaxed, and comfortable speaker who has a great story to tell. At our women-in-business event she confidently spoke of her personal journey while entertaining a highly engaged audience of 100+ people. Christelle received a warm response from her audience and the feedback we received about our speaker was all positive."

Cath Duncan
Board Chair, Anna Renie Chapter

"Christelle has wowed our audiences twice now. She has the gift of vulnerability and authority that takes people on a journey. When I hear the laughs from the crowd, I know a talk is going well and Christelle really delivers. Her zesty French accent certainly adds to the charm! If you're considering Christelle, she has my highest recommendation.

Glen Carlson
Director, Dent Global

"Our clients found her dynamic and she made them laugh, she was generous with sharing her own insights, tips and personal stories all with her endearing French accent! Christelle was prepared, on-time and executed to brief perfectly, I wouldn't hesitate to recommend her for similar speaking opportunities."

Sammi Jaeger
Program and Special Events Manager, Dent Global

"Very well organised and presented event. The information and insights provided to participants will make a difference to the way businesses approach their export activities.."

AusIndutry Masterclass Attendee